MW01233623

Train Travel through Europe

Europe by rail in twenty-six days. traveling to eleven countries and visiting 22 cities – London, Brussels, Antwerp, Amsterdam, Berlin, Wittenberg, Zurich, Budapest, Warsaw, Vienna, Milan, Paris, Venice, Florence, Rome, Bari, Thessaloniki, Athens, Corinth, Barcelona, Madrid, and New York

Conrad Birmingham

L W Birmingham and Sons LLC

Dedication

To my mother, JoAnn, for being so supportive through my medical problems.

Contents

Dedication 2

Preface...14

    Prayer My Illiness 16

Introduction..17

Trip Preparation 18

    Advice 1 – Plan Your Trip in Detail...18

    Advice 2 – Purchase a European Rail Pass.....................................19

    Advice 3 – Pay for First Class 19

    Advice 4 – Clothes..20

    Advice 5 – Travel App...20

Day 1 Jackson to Denver 21

    St. Louis..21

    Prayer European Trip..21

    Advice 6 – Google Flights 22

Day 2 Denver to London..23

    Denver..23

    Denver Airport 23

    On the Plane 23

Day 3 – London..25

    London 25

    Advice 7 – Public Transportation Cards...26

    Gatwick Airport 26

    Notting Hill 27

    Advice 8 – City Map Apps 28

    Notting Hill Hotel 28

    Prayer – Blood Clots...29

    Waterloo Station 30

    Westminster - House of Parliament 30

    Abraham Lincoln in Parliament Square...31

    Poem Abraham Lincoln 32

    Westminster Abby 33

St James Park 34

House Guard Parade Grounds..34

Buckingham Palace...35

St James Park – Bicycle Riding 36

Advice 9 - Bicycles 37

Fish and Chips 38

Advice 10 – Use your Debit or Credit Card to Pay 39

My Birthday Cake...39

Elevator!..39

Day 4 London...41

Bus Tour 41

Advice 11 – Hop On and Off Tour Buses 42

Tower of London 45

London Wall 5 AD 46

Tower Bridge 47

London Eye 48

St Paul's Cathedral 49

Shard 50

Poem Get as High as You Can..50

Advice 12 – Get as High as You Can 52

Prayer Success Trip...53

London's Summary 53

Day 5 On to Brussels 54

Eurostar to Brussels 54

Brussels 54

Grand Place...55

Advice 13 – Take Plenty of Pictures 55

Brussels wandering around..56

Real Belgium Waffles...60

Churches are the Tallest Buildings 61

Prayer Churches..61

Poem Churches 62

Advice 14 – Pick Up Snacks at a Market 64

Brussel's Summary 65

Antwerp..66

Bicycling Antwerp 66

Poem Bicycles..66

Advice 15 - Download Maps for City on to Cellphone.......68

Antwerp Picturesque..70

More bicycles...73

Advice 16 – Ask Directions...73

Day 6 Amsterdam 79

Amsterdam..79

On My Way to Amsterdam...79

Prayer Peace...79

Amsterdam Wandering Part 1..80

Advice 17 – Get a Cellphone Sims Card 80

American Breakfast with Baked Beans? 84

Poem Baked Beans 84

Amsterdam Wandering Part 2..85

Advice 18 – ATM's for Cash 85

Amsterdam Wandering Part 3..86

Amsterdam's Summary 91

Raining moved on to Dusseldorf and Frankfurt 92

Operation Market Garden 92

3rd Broken Train..93

Prayer Interrupted Travel Plans 93

Poem Three Broken Trains 93

Day 7 Whittenburg and Berlin 96

Wittenburg 96

Advice 19 - Visit Tourism Office 96

Martin Luther - Lutherans Wittenberg.................................96

Poem Martin Luther 98

Wittenberg's Summary 102

Prayer Martin Luther 102

Berlin 104

Berlin - Reichstag Survived WWII............................104

Berlin Train Terminal 108

Advice 20 - Take Pictures of Luggage 108

Berlin - Brandenburg Gate..110

Fifty-four Cranes in Berlin skyline...........................112

Advice 21 – Take a Walking Tour.............................113

Memorial to Murdered Jews 113

Prayer Holocaust...113

Poem Blocks of White 114

Soviet Military Monument 117

Poem Soviet Union 117

First Weather Issue - Cancelled Train 120

Berlin's Summary 121

Day 8 Zurich 122

Snow – Sleeping Car Cancelled................................122

Advise 22 - Be Flexible 122

Poem Girl on the Train 122

Zurich 124

Advice 23 - Make Copies of Passport 125

Zurich Train Station..125

Old Zurich...126

The Alps in the Distance..129

Fickle Weather 131

Zurich Harbor 131

Advice 24 – Bring Good Walking Shoes...................133

Zurich Churches..133

Zurich's Summary 137

Day 9 Budapest 138

  Budapest..138

    Budapest Train Station...138

    Poem - Gypsy 138

    Rough to Good 142

    Advice 25 – Patience 142

    Budapest on the River..146

    Starbucks is the New Travel Center. 150

    Advice 26 – Free Wi-Fi 151

    West Tennessee..152

    Budapest's Summary 153

    Prayer Budapest 153

Day 10 Warsaw 155

  Warsaw 155

    Warsaw Train Station 155

    Stroll to Warsaw Old City 157

    Advice 27 – Get Lost 157

    Warsaw Old Town 161

    Old City Wall...164

    Warsaw Ghetto 166

    Advice 28 – Say Yes..167

    Warsaw, before WWII, was a Home to the Jews 170

    Poem Immigration or Migration...................................170

    Poland Resistance - Printing Press...............................177

    Poem Resistance 177

    Young Fought in the Warsaw Uprising.........................178

    Warsaw's Summary 179

Day 11 Vienna 181

  Vienna...181

    Vienna Gigantic City - Bicycle It 181

    Vienna Wandering 186

Advice 29 – Act Like a Tourist 186

Shopping Area - Naschmarkt..188

Vienna Large River (Danube)..192

Advice 30 – Portable Power Bank Charger 193

Vienna's Summary 194

Miles of Vineyards...194

Day 12 Milan 196

Milan 196

Advice 31 – Read A History Book 196

Wandering Milan 196

Milan Wandering Part 2 203

Public Parks 206

Duomo Cathedral - Wow!..208

Prayer Duomo 209

Milan Castle 211

Advice 32 – Eat the Street Food 211

Milan Loves Dogs..215

Gigantic Graveyard..217

Milan - It is Friday!..221

Milan's Summary 221

Day 13 Paris 222

Paris..222

French Countryside 222

Advice 33 – Carry Ear Plugs and Eye Mask 222

Doing My Laundry 223

Prayer Laundry Mat 223

Advice 34 – City Attraction Cards 225

Arc de Triumph...225

Colonel Birmingham - "Stay out of crowds."..............................226

Eiffel Tower..228

Advice 35 – Keep Your Guard Up 228

River Seine...230

Excitement 232

Louvre...233

Cite - Notre De..236

Prayer Notre Da 237

Day 14 Paris...240

Bastille Market - Unbelievable!! 240

Paris More Wanderings 241

Advice 36 – Eat like the Locals....................241

Paris' Summary 245

More Alps 246

Day 15 Florence..247

Florence..247

Skipping Venice for now 247

Florence - Wandering 248

Advice 37 - Eat Main Meal for Lunch...........248

Florence Wandering 2 254

Advice 38 – Universal Travel Adaptor...........254

Overview Florence......................................257

Florence - Ponte Vecchino..........................259

Florence's Summary 260

Day 16 Rome 261

Rome..261

Advice 39 – Be Respectful 261

Rome Castle St Angelo................................262

Rome Colosseum..262

Rome Forum 263

Rome Pantheon..266

Rome St Peter's Cathedral 267

Advice 40 – Early Bird 268

Rome's Summary 269

Venice 269

   Advice 41 - Open Mind 270

   Venice - St Mark's Cathedral 270

   Venice Grand Canal 272

   Venice Shopping & Canals 274

   Venice's Summary 277

Day 17 Alps 279

  Alps 279

   Weird Rock Formations and Plenty of Vineyards 279

   Poem - Vineyards..279

   Wandering Alps 280

   Vineyards on the mountainside....................................281

   Hanging Out Here! 282

   Poem Alps 282

Day 18 Bari 284

  Bari 284

   More Port Bari 284

   An Excellent Way to Start the Day! 285

   Bari Wandering..286

   Advice 42 - Try New Food 287

   Lawn Control 287

   Castello Normanno Svevo 288

   Wow - fish, squid, oysters - fresh! 288

   Bari - Port Adriatic Sea..290

   City Wall - Walking, Bicycles, Houses 291

   More Port Bari 292

   Advice 43 – Download Google Translate......................292

   Inside City Walls 295

   Bari Sailing Club 298

   Bari - Roman Ruins 299

   Sundown Bari 301

Bari's Summary 302

Prayer Bari 302

Ferry Italy to Greece 302

Moon over the Adriatic Sea 304

Day 19 Greece..306

Greece 306

Greek Shoreline 306

Patras Landing 307

Tomorrow Apostle Paul's Travels 310

Prayer Apostle Paul's Trips 310

Sundown Greece 310

Athens Train Center 312

Day 20 Thessaloniki..315

Thessaloniki 315

Poem Thessalonica 315

Thessaloniki, My First Thought - Back in USSR 316

White Tower 318

Thessaloniki Wandering 320

Advice 44 – Be Open to Strangers...........................320

Poem - Erika 321

My Office - Starbucks...325

Thessalonica Wandering 2 327

Thessalonica's Market is Gigantic 329

Advice 45 – Haggle 329

Intercessory Prayer 332

Prayer – Intercessory Prayer 332

Advice 46 – Spontaneity...334

Paul Preached and Talked to Disciples.....................334

Poem Paul 334

Thessalonica Wandering 3 338

Byzantine Walls in Thessalonica..............................340

Poem Byzantine Empire 340

Thessalonica's Summary 345

Greeks are Very Patriotic - Flags...................................345

Day 22 Corinth..347

  Corinth 347

  Back to Corinth Tonight 347

  Present Day Corinth 347

  Ancient Corinth...349

  Corinth Canal and Ancient Corinth 352

  Corinth's Summary 356

  Athens 357

  Advice 47 – Join a Facebook Group of Cities to Visit 357

  Poem - Patriotic Day 357

  Acropolis...359

  Great Greek Lunch...362

  Advice 48 – Ask Hotel Staff for Recommendations 362

  Prayer Wonderful Meal 363

  Stoa Attalos 363

  Acropolis - Stadium 364

  Wandering Athens 366

  Wandering Athens 368

  Athens Skyline..371

  Athens Sunset 373

  Prayer Sunset 374

  Poem Sunset...374

Day 23 Athens...377

  Wading in the Aegean Sea...377

  Poem Sunrise 377

  Athens's Summary...379

  Barcelona 380

  Missed Barcelona..380

Poem - Cities Missed 380
Day 24 Madrid 382
  Madrid 382
    Advice 49 – Ask the Hotel for Upgrades 382
    Poem - Madrid 382
    Hop-On and Off Bus 384
    Wandering Madrid 386
    Catherdral de la Almudena 389
    Plaza de Mayor 391
    Advice 50 – Observe People Around You 391
    Palacio Real 392
    Don Quixote Statue 393
    Prayer Don Quixote 393
    Cortes Ingles View 395
    More Madrid Wandering 395
    Madrid's Summary 401
Day 26 New York 402
  New York 402
    Advice 51 – Splurge on a Taxi 402
    Prayer New York 402
    Poem - New York 402
    New York - World Trade Center 404
    Advice 52 – Pay Homage to National Tragedies ... 405
    Wandering New York 406
    Empire State Building 407
    New York's Summary 408
Flying Home New York to St Louis to Jackson 408
    Prayer Home Safe 409
Epilogue 410
About the Author 411
Appendix List of Travel Advice 412

Preface

I have had these mysterious symptoms for 4 or 5 years. I had the feeling that I was drugged up, floating, light-headed, dizzy, uneasy, discombobulated, and on occasion, fall backward without actually falling. I had seen 30 or more doctors in Jackson, Memphis, Nashville, Tennessee, and Rochester, Minnesota. I had visited Vanderbilt University Medical Center for several years. They told me to wait, and it will manifest itself in 10 to 15 years. I wondered if they were crazy. They did prescribe amitriptyline, which eliminated my mysterious symptoms for a few months, but my symptoms would come back. My last doctor in Tennessee was a neurologist in Memphis, and he would not touch me. He wrote on the medical records go to Mayo Clinic in Rochester, Minnesota. Mayo Clinic was the only clinic that could examine all of your complaints. The Mayo Clinic took all of the medical records from all of my doctors, including many, many examinations, MRI's, X-rays, blood tests, EKG's, and EMG's along with their added tests of inner ear tests, brain function tests, stress tests, and 24-hour blood pressure test. After four visits to the Mayo Clinic, the doctors eliminated many possible causes, including my heart, brain, skeletal system, nervous system, and inner ear. They did diagnose two causes of all my leg and hip pain but not my long-standing mysterious illness.

The first cause the Mayo Clinic identified was my right. My hip abductor was abnormally weak, causing my leg and hip pain every time I took one step. The pain was horrible. I hated to leave the house or to go anywhere. I did not want to walk into a store or around the park to walk my dog. I spent most of my time reading Christian books, especially the Bible, and watching the news. I would go to church every week, no matter how much the pain hurt me. I had to go to church to glorify God. I needed to be close to the Lord no matter how much pain I was in on that day. The pain made me irritable and a miserable person to be around. I am sure it caused a great deal of stress in my life, and I was probably depressed from all the pain. If a weak hip abductor caused all my pain, then that would be easy to remedy. I started a regiment of physical therapy, and in weeks my hip and leg quit hurting. They might be sore from exercising, but the pain was gone. Over half of my health problems had disappeared in weeks after 4 or 5 years. Praise God!

My mysterious illness was diagnosed as a generalized anxiety disorder. The doctor was an anxiety neurologist, and she was the only such doctor at the Mayo Clinic. Her solution was for me to change my medicine to Lexapro and to see a psychotherapist and psychiatrist. She believed I needed to be more in tune with my emotions, and I needed to take up cognitive behavior therapy, stress management techniques, and relaxation techniques. I changed to the new medicine, which has helped reduce my symptoms from every other day to a few times a month. The psychotherapist and psychiatrist were another matter. I disagreed that I was full of anxiety and depression. I was anxious and depressed when my leg hurt every day of the week for 4 or 5 years, but I did not feel that way now. I still wanted to test her theory, so I visited A Christian Counselor.

I visited an 81-year-old Christian Counselor who I saw for marriage counseling, relationship counseling, and divorce counseling. We talked for a while, and then she asked me: "Conrad, tell me about your daily routine." I told her I got up and drank coffee and caught up on the news. I would shave and clean up. For the next 2 hours, I would do the 20 to 30 exercises for my core and hip abductor, and every other day, I would go to the gym and lift weights. I would shower and eat lunch and then walk the dog. I told her that I would spend the afternoon reading and watching the news. Sometimes I would take a nap. I would eat supper and read or watch the news. During the day, I might go to the library, park, grocery store but spent a lot of time alone because I hated to walk. I quit all the volunteer work I did at the church because of the pain. After listening to my routine, she said, "You are not depressed, and you do not seem anxious." We talked about some other thing, and I asked her when I needed to come back. She said, "I cannot treat someone who is not depressed or anxious. She believed the doctors had nothing else to tell you, so this was the one thing that has not proven true or not." I agreed with her, and I shared that I would switch medicines. Also, I can visit her once a month. She said, "Sure, Joe, if you want to make an appointment, but I cannot help you if you do not need help."

Around this time, a new possibility presented itself, Progressive Supranuclear Palsy. I had eight of the twelve symptoms. I was walking down the symptoms just as they come to you if you have the disease. The disease is uncurable, and you waste away in a year. You end up not being able to eat, walk, or talk – a death sentence. The kicker is no one can tell you if you have it or not. There is no way to know until you die, and they do an autopsy. Doctors can then see the damage to your brain.

After suffering for so long, I decided this was my problem, and I needed to do some stuff in my life that I have always wanted to do. The first thing to come to my mind was a trip to Europe to see as much as possible while still walking and getting about. I planned a trip using the European railroad system.

This book is my story of touring Europe by its railroad system in twenty-six days. I traveled to eleven countries and visited 22 cities – London, Brussels, Antwerp, Amsterdam, Berlin, Wittenberg, Zurich, Budapest, Warsaw, Vienna,

Milan, Paris, Venice, Florence, Rome, Bari, Thessaloniki, Athens, Corinth, Barcelona, Madrid, and New York.

Prayer My Illiness

Wonder Father,

You know all and you are my strength. Watch over me and reduce the symptoms of my illness on this trip. Keep my cool and in control. I know you have this power and I ask it in the name of Jesus. Jesus has pardoned my sins and he ensures through my faith that I will be in heaven with you someday. Grant me these wishes if anything should go wrong.

In Jesus name I pray

Amen

I did not fall apart and waste away, which is good news because I would have Progressive Supranuclear Palsy. I am alive, living with my symptoms, and enjoying life.

Introduction

This book is my story of touring Europe by its railroad system in twenty-six days. I traveled to eleven countries and visited 22 cities – London, Brussels, Antwerp, Amsterdam, Berlin, Wittenberg, Zurich, Budapest, Warsaw, Vienna, Milan, Paris, Venice, Florence, Rome, Bari, Thessaloniki, Athens, Corinth, Barcelona, Madrid, and New York.

I wanted to travel light and fast. I planned to sleep on the train most of the time, renting a sleeping berth. I picked the order of cities to visit by how long the train ride would take and if it went overnight. I slept on my way to Berlin, Zurich, Budapest, Warsaw, Vienna, Milan, Paris, Venice, Thessaloniki, and Madrid. Every few days, I would stay in a hotel in a major city where I wanted to spend more time. I rented a room in London, Antwerp, Paris, Florence, Bari, Thessaloniki, Corinth, Athens, and Madrid. I slept one night on the ferry and the airplane from Athens to Barcelona. There was plenty of time to sleep.

I liked using the train because every train station was in the city center. I was dumped in the center of the city, where the city's historical culture is dominant. I placed my large bag in a locker at the train station, and I took my backpack with me. I started walking or caught a subway to the nearest Starbucks.

Yes, Starbucks was my office in every city. I would order my Americano and sit down and use their internet serviced. I would plan my day. Where I was going to walk and what I was going to visit. There was so much to see in each city, and I was visiting for one day, so I had to be on top of my game. I had to see as much as I could without getting bogged down in one place.

 I picked locations with spectacular views or great historical value. I ventured to all the major rivers or lakes in each city. I would take their local subway up and down the line to see more of the town and see people. I enjoyed watching people and their customs and attitudes.

The trip was an overview of Europe and its major cities. My journey did not disappoint.

Trip Preparation

I prepared for the trip by choosing the least expensive options as possible. I had limited cashflow, but I had plenty of time. Throughout the book I will be highlighting travel advice for a budget traveler. The trip was not glamorous, but it was exciting, and it was what I needed to do. Also, I saw all of Europe on this trip, so I planned very wisely.

The cost of the trip was roughly three thousand dollars with one thousand for the round trip tickets, seven hundred for the rail pass, five hundred for the hotels, and eight hundred for food and other things that might arise. If I had someone with me, I would have not kept a tight budget. I can be very frugal.

The main goal was to see the major cities of Europe in thirty days. I decided the best way to do this was to ride the train from city to city and sleep on the train for a few days to cover more ground. This worked fabulously. I traveled to the next city at night on the train ready the next morning to go right out into the city to see the historical city centers where most of the historical significance exits.

I started at the train station and I wandered the city trying to see the most important attractions, visiting any markets, and watching people. This worked out great and it was easy with most train stations in the historical parts of town and with subways it was even easier than I could imagine.

The second goal was to stop overnight at the major European cities such as London, Paris, Berlin, Rome, Athens, and Madrid. This enabled me to see more of these beautiful cities and it enabled me to shower and sleep comfortably. In some cases, I had to stay in a hotel because there were no night cars available to take me to the next stop. This is where the first advice come into our discussion. Plan your trip in detail.

Advice 1 – Plan Your Trip in Detail

I listed all the cities that I wanted to travel to and to explore. I studied the railroad maps in detail researching which ones had night cars traveling for 6 hours or more from one city to another city so I could sleep on the train. This was a key part of my journey. I learned a great deal preparing for this trip and it paid off the entire trip.

I learned that I could not get to Greece easily on the railroad, so I took a ferry from Bari, Italy to Patras, Greece. In reverse it was hard getting out of Greece, so I flew from Athens, Greece to Barcelona, Spain.

The second thing I learned was Greece's rail system was part of a rail pass, but you could not reserve seats because of Greece's economic troubles. There was nothing I could do about it, but it gave me some foresight on problems which might arise, and they did arise. Really, it was fun and exciting. More about that later when we reach Greece in the book.

Advice 2 – Purchase a European Rail Pass

The European Rail Pass enables you to travel on a train anywhere in Europe for one fee for a certain number of trips and days. This enabled you to make reservations ahead of time, so you knew that you had a seat, and you had a sleeper car. I was confused on which European Rail Pass was best, I chose eurail over raileurope. The main reason was eurail website was easier to use and understand. The prices were simpler.

Advice 3 – Pay for First Class

This was the best decision that I made on my trip. First Class allows you to sit in better seats with more amenities. The greatest amenity was charger's outlets for your phone. My phone needed to be constantly charged because of the posts that I was making on Facebook and Penguin (travel tracker), the usage of my maps to get around the cities, the internet to find interesting restaurants and historical sites, and the quantity of pictures that I was taking in each city. A few more amenities were free stacks in first-class, first-class restrooms (less people using them), and a better food menu then the regular train menu.

Advice 4 – Clothes

You must take limited clothes because you must carry them everywhere you go on the train. At the train depots there are lockers to place a suitcase into for the day, which is convenient, but you still must haul everything on and off the train. I took my favorite old man corduroy pants for warmth, a good pair of hiking boots, and good socks. I went in late winter in some countries and early spring in others. I rather be warm then cold. Pack one travel suitcase to leave in the train depot lockers and a good backpack to haul around as you toured the cities. This worked perfectly for me.

Advice 5 – Travel App

I used Penguin, a travel app, to document my trip. I posted pictures and stories about my trip. My friends could follow me on my trip. The app kept up with my location from my phone GPS. This created a great map of my trip. Also, at the end of the trip, I could print a book of my posts and pictures corresponding to the locations. I thought it was a great app and a provided great memory of my trip.

Day 1 Jackson to Denver

St. Louis

I spent the first day traveling from Jackson, Tennessee, to St. Louis, Missouri, and then to Denver, Colorado. I flew to St. Louis from Jackson on a little propeller plane. Traveling from Jackson has it advantages and the main one is you park thirty yards from the terminal. The disadvantages are it is hard to link up with flights out of St. Louis. You usually must wait a few hours. I did see a significant amount of flooding along the Mississippi River. The river was way over its banks. I have never seen that much flooding from the air.

Prayer European Trip

Dear Lord,

I am seeking your protection and blessings on this trip through Europe. Please, forgive me for my sins. I know that I am a sinner. You are mighty and wonderful. I know you will grant my prayers. Let me have a safe and peaceful trip.

In Jesus name I pray

Amen

When I got to St. Louis, I took the shuttle from the airport to downtown. I thought it would be cool to go downtown to the Gateway Arch. The trip was very unsafe with many youths or kids hanging out around the downtown stations with no purpose. I did not feel safe in downtown St. Louis. I checked out the Gateway Arch and I got out of there as soon as possible. I spent the next few hours in the airport. How boring. Finally, I was off to Denver. I spent the night in Denver to board my flight very early in the morning, Day 2.

The question is why Denver? I am going the wrong way. Well, I got a ticket that cost me $750 cheaper than taking a routine route. Yes, I lost a whole day, but I did not care. My cashflow was more important than time. I did get to see how dangerous St. Louis was to average person, I got to

21

see the flooding along the Mississippi River, and I go to see the Rockies in Denver. All in the first day.

I got a good airfare because I shopped on the discount airfare sites. My favorite is Google Flights, but you must do it in an incognito mode, or your airfares will go the next day if not sooner.

Advice 6 – Google Flights

There are so many advantages to using discount air apps to locate good inexpensive flights. Google Flight sis one of the best but make sure you search in incognito mode. You do not want to be tracked and pay more than you have to for tickets.

Day 2 Denver to London

Denver

March 5, 2019, in the United States, Denver International Airport, Leaving today and getting there tomorrow – my birthday. Happy Birthday to me. In Denver, I saw was the Rookies in the distance, a hotel room, and an airport.

Denver Airport

Always something!

March 5, 2019, in the United States, the Denver International Airport. My doctor's office called as I was boarding the plane. The medicine that they gave me does not cover the infected cyst on my back. Now, I got to find a pharmacist in London. What a pain.

On the Plane

I met a lovely woman who plays the harp. We talked about Jesus' good old religious songs. She had some odd beliefs about the 5th Dimension, but I politely listened to her. She was a nice person.

I like to listen to people about their spiritual beliefs. I am very evangelistic, and I like to share the gospel without being too forceful or impolite. I find it is easier to listen and to pray for an opening to share Jesus. God is in control and God will make it happen if that is His will. I want to be obedient to Him.

The plane was cramped, and I got up every two hours to walk about and do calf raises. I did not want to get a blood clot on this long flight.

Day 3 – London

London

Yes, a long flight from Denver to London. I was excited to be in Europe. I had been to Amsterdamam and Frankfurt, passing through on an airplane. I was not a tourist. I had been to Moscow and Arkhangelsk in Russia, and I was a tourist at the same time adopting my children, Michael and Samantha. Moscow was interesting and exciting, while Arkhangelsk was a factory town. There was nothing to see in the city of 500,000, but the countryside was fascinating. The scenery was rustic and beautiful with snow.

Arkhangelsk is nothing like London. London is full of things to see and do. It is similar to Moscow for the number of things to see and do, but the atmosphere is different. Moscow was still recovering from the breakup of the Soviet Union. The interpreter was paranoid of KBG and big brother watching us all the time. The citizens did not speak as much English as you thought they might, but we were in Russia. On the second trip, the terrorists, Chechens, were causing many problems, and we were stopped five or six times. They took us out of our car, and we had to show our passports. Our guide lets us know if there are more than three people in a vehicle, they will stop you. We were not allowed to explore Moscow the second time that we visited Moscow. They were terrified for our safety. I did not feel this way at all in London.

I was able to travel everywhere in London with no feeling of dread or impending disaster. Like any large city, you have to use common sense, and the perils lurk out there, but the atmosphere was bright and bubbly. I could feel people were upbeat and alive. As soon as I got off the airplane at the airport, I could feel the energy.

I arrived at Gatwick Airport in early March, and it was early in the morning. The weather was cloudy and overcast. I went to the underground station, Piccadilly, to catch a train to downtown London.

The first thing that I had to do is to get an Oyster card. You can buy a travel card and preload it with money. You can travel on any transportation options, bus, underground, and train. This is a must to get to London, so stop at the airport and pick up an Oyster Card.

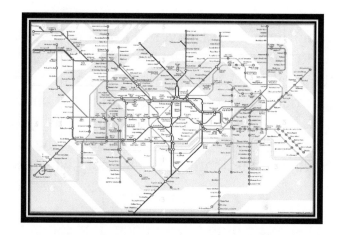

Advice 7 – Public Transportation Cards

In most major cities, you can purchase a mass transit pass to pay for the trips. Usually it will save you money, but it is very convenient to have an easy payment system instead of carrying the right cash and change. Also, you can jump from metro systems to buses very easy with the mass transit cards. You must purchase them in every city it is so much easier.

I had to get to Tower Bridge Station to transfer to the line that would take me to Notting Hill Gate station.

The tube station was busy. The regular airport traffic and the early morning rush to work for many resulted in mass confusion. I was glad that I was by myself or worried about the people with me. I would have fretted about losing them. There were so many people. This is the moment you think of being pushed off the landing into the oncoming train. I have watched too many movies.

Gatwick Airport

March 6, 2019, in the United Kingdom, Gatwick Airport

I experienced my first broken train at the airport. Fifteen to thirty minutes and it was remedied. I took the train to the Tower Bridge underground station and then caught a subway or tube to Notting Hill

Notting Hill

March 6, 2019, in the United Kingdom, Notting Hill Gate Going to hotel drop bag. Then out and about.

Now the tricky part, I had studied how to perform this maneuver, and I knew it would be confusing and chaotic. Yes, it was all that and more. I was a little punch drunk from the long trip, so it was hard to get my bearings. I am glad that I downloaded the Citymapper for my android phone. Once I got on the train, I could sit down and open the app, and study on it. I knew where I was going, but it gave me a little more comfort.

Advice 8 – City Map Apps

This is anither innovation thanks to smart phones. Download city map apps to your phone as soon as possible. They are connected to mass transportaion and tourist sites. If you are walking, it makes seeing al of the historical sites simple.

I made it to Tower Bridge station and transferred to the District line to get to Notting Hill. Notting Hill was the location that I had picked out for my stay. Everyone remembers the movie Notting Hill and the warm, good vibes it gave you. I understand it is a movie, and it was planned and acted out to perfection. Everything turns out rosy pink in the end, and is that not what we want for our lives. I think so.

I arrived at Notting Hill Gate, and my room was a short walk down Kensington Church Street. Kensington Church Street is full of shops. The street is lined with coffee shops, little bars, antique shops, and boutiques. I enjoyed my walk down the road soaking up the atmosphere.

Notting Hill Hotel

March 6, 2019, in the United Kingdom, Notting Hill Gate is excellent and convenient. I checked in early and crashed. My leg swelled up. Awful. 2-hour nap just like new. Long-distance plane flights are going to have to be avoided. I was saying.

At times it was hard to enjoy the moment with your suitcase banging against your leg, but it was ok. I was in London and one hundred yards from my room for two days.

I made it to the room and checked in quickly. The stairways were tiny and made for someone else than a size 13 shoe. I felt like I was tiptoeing up the stairs. The room was what I expected small, but it would do. There was a bed and a bathroom. What else do you need? I laid on the bed right away. My leg was killing me. I had developed a blood clot on the flight from the United States.

My blood clot count was up to eight and always in the same place below my knee, right between my knee and calf. I have a blood disorder, Factor Five. I get blood clots sporadically. After the first blood clot, when I had a hip replacement, it became a possibility.

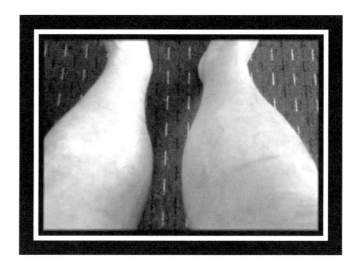

Prayer – Blood Clots

    Lord,

Please give me relief from these awful blood clots. You are my God and I need your help. You are the creator of the heavens and the earth and you knitted me. Please he me.

In Jesus name I pray

Amen

I took blood thinner, and I am cautious about exercising and about walking frequently. Every time I went to the Emergency Room, nothing would happen. They would perform an ultrasound and say go home. What I hated was it cost $3,000. I quit going to the emergency room because nothing ever came from the visit. Maybe I am playing Russian roulette with my blood clots. I know they can be deadly, but the medical community has done nothing to address them, so why will I.

This time is different. I learned to take an extra aspirin and walk on my leg to pump the blood out of my calf.

Waterloo Station

March 6, 2019, in the United Kingdom, Westminster Abbey

I took the underground from Notting Hill to Waterloo and wandered from there. The underground is so busy and noisy.

Everyone is in a hurry. They are so busy living.

Westminster - House of Parliament

March 6, 2019, in the United Kingdom, Big Ben and Parliament Building

Abraham Lincoln in Parliament Square

March 6, 2019, in the United Kingdom, Whitehall.

I was stunned that Abraham Lincoln's statue was here in Parliament Square. United States citizens have reverence for Abraham Lincoln, but I did not know the British took him as seriously as we do. What an honor for him to be here in this prominent location.

Poem Abraham Lincoln

What are you doing in London
Where they have many to honor
Have the British sunken
Honoring an Amerikaner

A white dude
From the United States
Who defeated an internal feud
Changing all our fates

Keeping us as one
Freeing the slaves
By military might and the gun
Sending many to their graves

A strong man of high ideals
Full of integrity
As history reveals
He conquered our greatest enemy

Bigotry

Prejudice
Racism
Intolerance

A good leader
Leading our nation
A good cheerleader
Defending our foundation

Our foundation on individual rights
And individual liberties
Taking us to new heights
And endless possibilities

I can understand and comprehend
Why any country would let him stand
As a statue and as their friend
In any nation or land

Westminster Abby

March 6, 2019, in the United Kingdom, Westminster Abbey

St James Park

March 6, 2019, in the United Kingdom, St James's Park Green, St James Park. Excellent area to ride bicycles.

House Guard Parade Grounds

March 6, 2019, in the United Kingdom, Horse Guards Parade

Buckingham Palace

March 6, 2019, in the United Kingdom, Green Park Buckingham Palace

St James Park – Bicycle Riding

March 6, 2019, in the United Kingdom, St James's Park

A great bicycle trail from Parliament to St James Park across to Green
Park with dedicated bicycle lanes. I enjoyed this bicycle ride, and it was
pretty fun. A little windy and cold, but a good experience.

Advice 9 - Bicycles

A bicycle is the best way to see any city. There are bicycle trails, and you can move around the city from tourist location to tourist location. Most cities have bicycles that you can rent right from a rack, or you can telephone a bicycle shop. The bicycle shops will deliver them to you at a hotel or a specific location. I cannot emphasis how much fun it is to ride a bicycle as you tour a city.

Fish and Chips

I went back to Notting Hill, and it was dinner time. I was starving after a long day walking and biking around London. I wanted something specifically from London, so I thought of fish and chips. The restaurant that I picked served fish and chips.

March 6, 2019, in the United Kingdom, Notting Hill Gate Dinner traditional fish and chips. Top ten fish and chip London.

Advice 10 – Use your Debit or Credit Card to Pay

Most debit and credit cards will convert from a foreign currency to the dollar. It is easier for you to pay the bill in the local currency with your bank card instead of carrying the foreign currency or letting the local establishment set the exchange rate. It is usually higher than normal.

My Birthday Cake

March 6, 2019, in the United Kingdom, Notting Hill Gate salted caramel ice cream with free Wi-Fi.

I celebrated my birthday, too.

Elevator!

March 6, 2019, in the United Kingdom, Notting Hill Gate, My great grandfather's (Conrad Hanafee) elevator was this big in Jackson. In his house. Hahaha

Day 4 London

Bus Tour

March 7, 2019, in the United Kingdom, Whitehall

Bus Tour around London and Thames River

I followed my medical advice, and I got up. I walked to the Hop-on Hop-Off Bus Tour stop in Notting Hill. I had purchased a ticket which cost $50.00, and it was the easiest way to explore London. London has so much to see and to do, and I had to get my bearings. A Hop-on Hop-Off Bus was the best way. The tour includes a map and headphones. The headphones were fabulous in telling the stories of London.

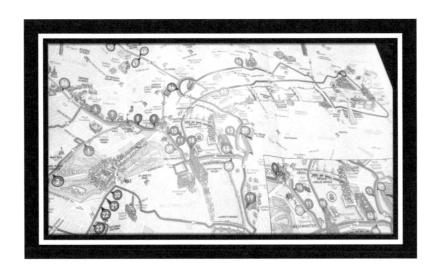

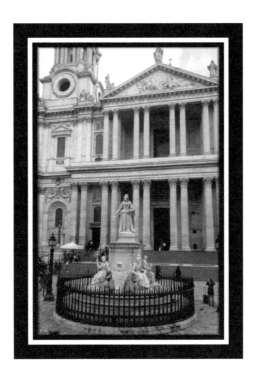

Advice 11 – Hop On and Off Tour Buses

Hop on and off tour buses are an excellent way to see a city
if you have little time or if you want an overview of the city.
They give a good tour of the city with plenty of historical
references and explanations.

Tower of London

March 7, 2019, in the United Kingdom, The Tower of London

Tower of London

London Wall 5 AD

March 7, 2019, in the United Kingdom, The Tower of London

Next to the Tower of London is a wall built by Romans.

Tower Bridge

March 7, 2019, in the United Kingdom, Tower Bridge

London Eye

March 7, 2019, in the United Kingdom, London Eye Time

St Paul's Cathedral

March 7, 2019, in the United Kingdom, St Paul's Cathedral

Shard

March 7, 2019, in the United Kingdom, London Bridge Railway Station.

A great view of London from the observation platform. This is a must see attraction to observe London. Besides the bus tour around London, this was my favorite attraction.

Poem Get as High as You Can

This is not about smoking a joint
But when you are touring
Get to the highest point
The views are enduring

The view of the cities are marvelous
And it is not to be missed
You will not feel purposeless
Giving you a high or gigantic lift

To see the city spread out
The civilization of man
This is what it is all about
We are no longer caveman

The high point could be a building
A tall skyscraper
That you feel is tilting
If you fell they would need a scrapper

To clean you off the ground
At a gigantic height
Where you can see all around
A sure blessing at night

With all the lights
A lit up Christmas tree
Producing different panoramic sites
A blessing for all to see

The overlook could be a mountaintop
Or a large hill
Which could be along drop
But it is definitely a thrill

The view can be a tourist trap
Made as an attraction
And tighten your bootstrap

There is a lot of walking action

But they all have a tremendous view
I wish I could fly
And I would have flew
Because it is extremely high

Advice 12 – Get as High as You Can

Find the tallest building or hill I the city and go there. You
get the best views of the city and usually it is breath taking.

Prayer Success Trip

Dear God,

You are wonderful. My trip is going f=good and I give you the credit to make things run smoothly. Thank you for watching over me and letting me have sucha good time.

In Jesus name I pray

Amen

London's Summary

London was everything that I expected it to be. I enjoyed seeing all these places that I read about in history books. The weather was what I expected too – cloudy and dreary. I think you need a week or two to see all the sights in London and the surrounding area.

Day 5 On to Brussels

Eurostar to Brussels

March 8, 2019, in the United Kingdom, St Pancras International Railway Station

I purchased a ticket early for the Eurostar because they can sell out quickly. I left London on the Eurostar for continental Europe. The Eurostar is swift, and fast. We were in France in no time. I was traveling through France to the Belgium visit Brussels.

Brussels

Brussels is the capital and largest city of Belgium. It is located in the central part of the country. I wouldn't say I liked Brussels. It was pretty and exciting but, I did not feel comfortable when I got off the train and walked to the main tourist areas. Maybe it was the police officer saying, watch your stuff? Brussels and Amsterdam had police officers telling you to watch your bags.

This stayed with me the whole time I was in Brussels. I was looking over my shoulder the whole time. I think Brussels was the only place in Europe where I did not feel safe.

I put my heavy bag in a locker at the train station and took off toward the main tourist area.

Once I had gone half a mile, everything became safer. As I wandered in the main squares and the leading shops. I set out down the Rue de Neuve which is the main street. There a plenty of shops and resturants along with tourist.

Grand Place

March 8, 2019, in Belgium, Grand Place Brussels

There were many restaurants and shops here. I liked shopping for chocolates and the toy soldiers caught my interest..

Advice 13 – Take Plenty of Pictures

You want to take as many pictures as you can especially since they do not have to be developed and printed by the roll. I know kids do not get this, but it was a hassle and expensive. I am amazed at the pictures that I have created and the wonderful scenes and scenery. Just snap picture after picture and wait to find out what you have captured digitally. At night, I would go through my pictures eliminating the bad ones or duplicates.

Brussels wandering around

Real Belgium Waffles

March 8, 2019, in Belgium, Galleries Royales Saint-Hubert

I had to try a Belgium waffle and I got a Keffer something or another. I have been waffles all my life, so I wanted a genuine one form their birth place. The Keffer was a sausage, and it was good too.

I sat in a restaurant along the main tourist boulevard and watched people for a few hours. It is fun to watch and to observe.

Churches are the Tallest Buildings

March 8, 2019, in Belgium, De Collinte

In little towns between Brussels and Antwerp, the churches are the tallest buildings with canals stretching for miles. The canals are straight as they can be.

Prayer Churches

Dear Mighty one

You are wonderful and great, and the populace of Europe knows this too. Your churches litter the landscape, and your presence is known. Forgive us for our sins and help us to make you relevant in our lives every day.

In Jesus name I pray

Amen

Poem Churches

In the olden days
Churches were prominent.
And worthy of praise
They were dominant

The center of a town
The highest peak
A glorious crown
A sanctuary for the weak

You could see them for miles
Standing tall on the skyline
Encouraging our lifestyles
A Godly and righteous sign

Packed full every Sunday
With worshippers who cared
Where they would pray
So they can be spared

A life of torment

In the prison of hell
Instead of the ascent
To a heavenly dwell

What has happened
The churches are still there
But I am saddened
Empty it would appear

Have people lost their hope
And have they lost their belief
Not only Europe but the globe
Now how do they get relief

Relief from their sins
And their grief
Or celebrate their wins
And kill the fatted beef

I do not know
But churches fill up
When there is a major blow
They remember the body and cup

When there is too much
For them to understand
It is their crutch
But it is made of sand

God is in you
We are the temple
Jesus knew
The Holy Spirit is central

To be in your heart
Day after day
You do not need a royal court
To handle the fray

God is there

Right inside
Do not shed a tear
You are His bride

Married to Christ
And to all it brings
He was sacrificed
As scripture sings

To give you life
And give you peace
To end your strife
And your unbelief will cease

Advice 14 – Pick Up Snacks at a Market

I recommend purchasing snacks at a local market that you may pass. Snacks can be expensive in train stations and on trains and many times not available or food establishments not open. Also, if you are wandering a city it is easier to snack on something handy in your backpack instead of stopping for a meal.

Brussel's Summary

I enjoyed Brussels. There were a nice downtown area walking distance of the train station with plenty of shops and eateries. I had no expectations of Brussels, so I was not disappointed or enlightened by the city. A quaint city with a nice, concentrated tourist area.

Antwerp

Antwerp is a port city in the northern part of Belgium and is the second-largest city in the country. Antwerp's old town, has medieval and Renaissance architecture and it, is a popular tourist attraction.

I wanted to stop here because of its tremendous bicycle trails located around the city and along the river.

When I arrived, the train station is close to the old town, so it was easy to walk to the center of town. I ventured down the Meir into the historical center of town.

Bicycling Antwerp

March 8, 2019, in Belgium, Antwerp

Poem Bicycles

We know them from our youth
Almost everyone rode a bike
But let me tell you the truth
It is better than a long hike

I can tour a city
Much quicker

Without pity
As I watch and snicker

Those who are walking
Shuffling their feet
Knees knocking
Down the street

Walking is slow
And it is hard
In my grand show
Bicycling is my face card

I can move place to place
Many miles a part
With much grace
Remembering by heart

The simple motions to ride
A little forward push
Begin to glide
Then sit on your tush

Reach to the pedals
And pump your legs
You may not earn any medals
Or turn any heads

But you are moving
Without swinging your hips
You are crusing
Ready for many trips

I love to bicycle. I had a great time. I got to see a lot of the city and I got lost. I went out of my way ten miles. A friendly kid rented a bicycle and took me back to where I belonged. Ha-ha.

Advice 15 - Download Maps for City on to Cellphone

I had a map of the city, but it was not in detail. It gave the major attractions and bicycle route but not every street, so it got to be confusing. Next time, I will download most city maps on my cellphone, so I have a map available if I do not have wi-fi or the map is inferior to what I need.

The bicycle routes were amazing with two tunnels under the river at each end of the city. The tunnels had elevators and escalators. How cool is that. What a bicyclist paradise.

Antwerp Picturesque

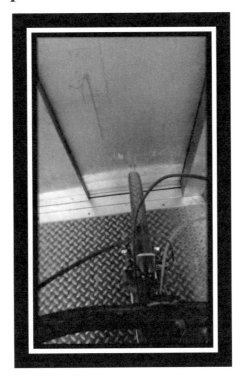

March 8, 2019, in Belgium, Universiteit Antwerpen / Prinsstraat Beautiful city.

So many nooks and crannies to explore. I see similarities to Quebec City. Quebec City was friendly with old, old city flavor, but Antwerp has it beat. I think it would take a week to find all the little squares with shops hidden here and there. There is gigantic diamond market here too.

More bicycles

March 8, 2019, in Belgium, Antwerpen-Centraal station

There is a good bicycle shop at the train station. It was easy to rent a bicycle and they were everywhere. People riding with bags from shopping, kids riding their bicycles just out playing, racers hurrying around going fast, and commuters just going home.

Advice 16 – Ask Directions

I was riding my bicycle to the river, and I missed a turn. I think I rode twenty minutes further then I was supposed to go but I was lost. I could not figure out how to get to the river by the map and I was going to have to back track a long way to find the right path.

I asked a kid on the bicycle if he knew the way to the river. We had a hard tie communicating but he waved for me to follow him. He took me to the river, and it had to be out of his way. He was such a nice kid and so generous with his time.

Sometimes just ask directions instead of being frustrated and lost.

Antwerp's Summary

I love Antwerp. There are plenty of bicycle trails on both sides of the river and miles outside the city. Also, the downtown area was concentrated around a few centralized blocks and after work there were hundreds of people out and about. They were riding bicycles, dining in cafes and shopping in many stores. I liked this because it was not a weekend. This was a week day and in the early evening the people just came out onto the streets.

I would spend more time here if I had a chance, maybe three or four days.

Day 6 Amsterdam

Amsterdam

Amsterdam is the capital and largest city of the Netherlands, I wanted to visit Amsterdam because of its beautiful canals, historic architecture, and cultural rumors or scene. Amsterdam has a rich history dating back to the 17th century when it was one of the most important ports in the world, and there are stories from history of its historical significance. Their navies ruled the oceans for years settling far off countries and continents even New York.. I wanted to meet these people.

I wanted to observe the red district and the pot houses so popular on television and in movies. Is it true or just an exaggeration.

Also, Amsterdam is a popular tourist destination with many museums especially the Van Gogh Museum. He led the impressionist movement, and his paintings are phenomenal.

Amsterdam is also known for its bicycling culture, and it's considered one of the most bike-friendly cities in the world. I think Antwerp will have them beat but we will see.

On My Way to Amsterdam

March 9, 2019, in the Netherlands, Station Breda,

I had 10 hours of good sleep. Now, off on the train to Amsterdam. Very quiet. The train is empty on Saturday. New country Netherlands. The police officer said bye and said, watch your bag. How unnerving when it is the first thing you hear when you get off the train.

Prayer Peace

Dear Beloved Father,

Watch over me and protect me from those who would want to do me harm. I know you are mighty, and you know all. Send me on a different path then those seeking troubles.

In Jesus name I pray

Amen

Amsterdam Wandering Part 1

March 9, 2019, in the Netherlands, Rembrandtplein

I wandered down the Damrak to the Dam Square. There are hundreds of shops up and down the canal and down various allies. It would take weeks to venture into every nook and cranny.

Advice 17 – Get a Cellphone Sims Card

I purchased a cellphone Sims card in Amsterdam for Europe. I did not get it in London because their sim cards were for Great Britain or Brussels because I did not feel safe there but try to get it as soon as you can. Also, I had a dual sim card cellphone, so I plugged the second sim right into my cellphone. I was able to use the internet for directions a lot easier than finding a wi-fi spot. The sim card was very inexpensive.

American Breakfast with Baked Beans?

March 9, 2019, in the Netherlands, Rembrandtplein

I was very hungry when I got off the train and I saw a sign genuine American breakfast. I ordered the breakfast, and it came with baked beans. I have never had baked beans with my bacon and eggs. It must be an English or Canadian thing.

Poem Baked Beans

I have eaten a lot of baked beans
With hamburgers and hotdogs
Especially in my teens
But I never read it in travelogs

Baked beans for breakfast
Is what they advertised
An American breakfast was prefaced
And was I surprised

And to my astonishment
My breakfast came out
I was not overconfident
And I had my doubt

And I was right
Baked beans is not traditional
Here it was in my sight
But I am sure it is nutritional

They had eggs and bacon
And orange juice and toast too
Now we are takin
But baked beans who knew

For breakfast before
Or for breakfast ever since
And I swore
Because it made me wince

Amsterdam Wandering Part 2

March 9, 2019, in the Netherlands, Rembrandtplein

Advice 18 – ATM's for Cash

In today's society, you do not have to carry a large sum of cash because there are ATM's everywhere where you can get cash. It is better than hiding your cash in a sock. Before you leave home, make sure you have a no fee bank card.

Amsterdam Wandering Part 3

March 9, 2019, in the Netherlands, Oud-West

Amsterdam's Summary

I can see how people love Amsterdam. The canals and connecting bridges with houses lining the canals is picturesque. There were plenty of shops and eateries and I will always remember baked beans for breakfast. A true American breakfast in Amsterdam.

This is another city to visit for a week. You can get lost wondering the canals for days or a bicycle might be easier.

I cut my trip short because of rain and moved on.

Raining moved on to Dusseldorf and Frankfurt

March 9, 2019, in the Netherlands, Overberg

Amsterdam rain, so I added Dusseldorf and Frankfurt. A global pass, I can get on any train in Europe and go somewhere. I did not make it to these cities because the train broke down three times.

Operation Market Garden

March 9, 2019, in the Netherlands, Arnhem Railway Station

In World War II the British forces were trapped and surrounded here in Operation Market Garden. One too many bridges to capture and hold for a rush into the Germany. If it were not raining, I would have jumped off the train and checked out the city. . Heroes died here and it would have been nice to view the area that I had read about in books.

3rd Broken Train

March 9, 2019, in Germany, Steegh

A third broken train with rain and a double rainbow.

Prayer Interrupted Travel Plans

Dear Lord,

You are good and wonderful. Please, help me to keep on track and to make my next train. You know all and no the train troubles that we are presented with today. Give me and grace and get me to the next station on time.
In Jesus name I pray

Amen

Poem Three Broken Trains

They say things come in threes
But I was surprised
The trains did not run with a breeze
Or how advertised

Run like clock work
But not in this case
Unusual according to the clerk
In a limited time and space

Three broke down
Within a few hours
Makes you want to frown
As we sat in the rain showers

Three on one line
They were quite excited
Here near the Rhine

Problems uninvited

All you could do is wait
Make the best of it
Like lost freight
We would be found in a bit

But you do not find time
Lost due to train troubles
Barely had time
I had to march on the double

To make my next train
A sleeper for the night
My schedule I need to maintain
It will be alright

Frankfurt was missed
Just one municipality
I was not pissed
Just train life normality

There will be hitches
And unforeseen circumstances
Just hit the pitches
And take your chances

Day 7 Whittenburg and Berlin

Wittenburg

I arrived in Whittenburg after a thirty to forty minute train ride from Berlin. It was late at night, and I took a taxi to my hotel. The train station is a good fifteen minutes from downtown Whittenburg.

I woke up early and I set out to hike about Whittenburg. I wanted to walk in the footsteps of Martin Luther to see what kind of town produced such an influential man. I do not think it took more than thirty minutes to circle the town and the old town central is very compartmentalized in a small area.

Whittenburg is a little town with no grand features except the church where martin Luther posted the 95 Articles on the Castle Church.

I am glad that I ventured here to see the place where the Protestant Reformation started in the 1400's.

Advice 19 - Visit Tourism Office

Every city has a tourism office, and it is a good idea to visit theses offices. They usually have maps and lists of walking tours, bus tours, and other tours. Also, they have free advice, and they are knowledgeable about their city and what tourist like to do. This is a good place to start when you get to a city.

Martin Luther - Lutherans Wittenberg

March 10, 2019, in Germany, Lutherstadt Wittenberg Hbf City of Lutherhaus Wittenberg –

Martin Luther lived and taught here. He started the Protestant Reformation here by posting his proclamation against the Catholic Church and the Pope on the door of the church.

Poem Martin Luther

He started the Protestant Reformation
By studying the scripture
Not according to his station
He looked at a different picture

The Catholic Church
Believed it was right
And it carried the torch
Of Gods might

Luther believed we were vessels
Our oneness with Christ

Not layers or levels
Jesus made the sacrifice

For you and me
For our sin
And this set us free
New in our skin

Depending upon Jesus
For our salvation
Not indulgences to please us
Jesus was our causation

No matter how much I worked
Jesus was the only way
Not how little I shirked
Or how much to pay

I could not seek justification
From payments for atonement
To save us from damnation
Jesus was our proponent

Luther changed the power play
Not relying on man
Or their decisions in shades of gray
He understood the scripture was Gods plan

It was the truth
Black and white
The book from our youth
Which explains our plight

So treasure the Bible
Depending upon the Word
Do not be libel
Or follow the herd

99

Wittenberg's Summary

Very interesting, to walk in the steps of Martin Luther. The town elders have kept most of the city authentic. A day or two would be enough to wander Wittenberg especially with Berlin so close.

My only fault is they built a new train station and it is a long way from the town center. You have to rent a taxi to get back and forth.

Prayer Martin Luther

Dear Holy One,

You are ever knowing, and you knew what we needed and when we need it. Thank you for empowering Martin Luther to read and understand your scripture and to share his revelations to us. We know the work of the Holy Spirit was strong in him and make it strong in us.

In Jesus name I pray

Amen

Berlin

Berlin is the capital of Germany and it's a big city with lots to see and do. It's located in the northeastern part of the country, right by the River Spree. The city has a pretty interesting history - it was the capital of Prussia the German Empire, and Nazi Germany. Once Nazi Germany surrounded to the ally nations it was divided for the duration of the Cold War. When the Soviet Union fell, West (allies) and East Germany (communist) were reunited as one nation.

As a kid, I remember meeting all the World War II veterans who fought in World War II and the sacrifices they made for the United States. Also, I remember all the tension of the Cold War even practicing air raids in case of a nuclear war. I wanted to see Berlin because it has been at the center of most major conflicts for the past one-hundred and fifty years.

 Nowadays, Berlin is known for being a lively and diverse city with loads of cool stuff to check out, like the Brandenburg Gate and the Berlin Wall. It's also home to loads of museums, art galleries, and parks. It is supposed to be s a popular spot for students, artists, and young people, which I am none of, but it would be cool to look around Berlin especially memories from my youth.

I got off the train and I ventured toward the Reichstag, and I ended up on Unter den Linden. I think it was the main street in downtown Berlin, but it was not tourist as most cities. I wandered further into Berlin.

Berlin - Reichstag Survived WWII

March 10, 2019, in Germany, Panke

Reichstag has been Germany's government center for years except during the occupation of Germany by Allied Forces after WWII. It became the government center again in the early '90s. The dome on top is a tourist attraction allowing you to see for miles and miles around Berlin.

104

Berlin Train Terminal

March 10, 2019, in Germany, Berlin Hauptbahnhof

The new terminal is gigantic. It is a mall inside with many shops and eateries. Trams, local trains, national trains, and international trains come and go. It is located around the German government buildings.

The train station is a short walk to the main tourist attractions. I did not have to find a trolley or bus. It was a nice stroll on a cloudy day.

Advice 20 - Take Pictures of Luggage

You need a picture of your luggage. I did not lock my locker correcting in the Berlin train terminal and it was turned into lost and found. They were worried someone will steal it and I am glad for these good citizens.

I was able to show lost and found my luggage picture and it reduced the hassles of telling them what was inside my luggage – shirts, underwear, etc..

Berlin - Brandenburg Gate

March 10, 2019, in Germany, Brandenburg Gate

The gate symbolized the Cold War. Unrestrained capitalist vs. Communist's, planned economies. Communist were not free It was all for the state, all share the wealth, take from wealthy, and give it to the poor. The communist believed they can run things better or more just. Capitalism let the individual man choose what to make and what to buy. There was no planned economies just market forces set by what people wanted to buy and scarcity of what they wanted to buy.

There was a wall dividing East (communist) and West Berlin (capitalism). In my late 20's or the early 1990's the Soviet Union fell apart and all its satellite nations were dismantled, and they became individual nations. The symbol of tyranny or communism "the gate" is a tourist attraction. No wall and no Soviet Union but there are tourist and memories..

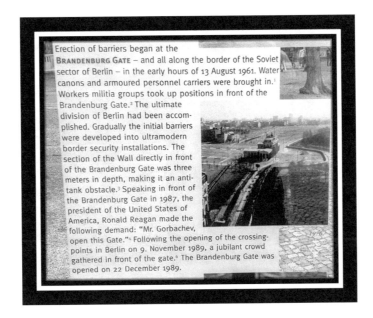

Erection of barriers began at the BRANDENBURG GATE – and all along the border of the Soviet sector of Berlin – in the early hours of 13 August 1961. Water canons and armoured personnel carriers were brought in.[1] Workers militia groups took up positions in front of the Brandenburg Gate.[2] The ultimate division of Berlin had been accomplished. Gradually the initial barriers were developed into ultramodern border security installations. The section of the Wall directly in front of the Brandenburg Gate was three meters in depth, making it an anti-tank obstacle.[3] Speaking in front of the Brandenburg Gate in 1987, the president of the United States of America, Ronald Reagan made the following demand: "Mr. Gorbachev, open this Gate."[4] Following the opening of the crossing-points in Berlin on 9. November 1989, a jubilant crowd gathered in front of the gate.[5] The Brandenburg Gate was opened on 22 December 1989.

Fifty-four Cranes in Berlin skyline

March 10, 2019, in Germany, Berlin Hauptbahnhof

I count cranes. Yes, I count cranes because it is a sign of the economy, and sometimes it means the city is getting overbuilt. I have seen 5 to 10 cranes all over Europe, but 54 cranes in Berlin - oh my. Last time that I saw more than ten cranes was in Nashville over the past two years and Miami before the crash in 2006. There were bunches of cranes in Miami.

Advice 21 – Take a Walking Tour

A walking tour is a good way to visit the main tourist sights and to learn a great deal about the city. They are available many times per day, and it will give you a good orientation and background of the city.

Memorial to Murdered Jews

March 10, 2019, in Germany, Holocaust Memorial

An interesting memorial to the murdered Jews is right in the center of Berlin. It has every one of the Jews killed from 1933 to 1945. The American Embassy is next to the memorial.

Prayer Holocaust

Dear God,

I will never understand this misery and suffering opposed on a body of people because of their beliefs. I believe it is for your glory that things happen and someday may I know the rest of the story. Not for this one massacre for the endless massacres throughout the world including wars and abortions. I know that I am a sinner and you are without sin. Please forgive my questioning soul for not trusting you and

112

your plans. You are mighty and the creator of all – thank you Lord..

In Jesus name I pray

Amen

I get goosebumps thinking about how many human beings were killed for no other reason than they were Jews who practiced a different religion. A mad, fanatic leader demonized them and made them the problem. They were the problem for everything. How easy this could happen today with the mass media control of the narrative. Very scary.

Poem Blocks of White

In Berlin
Near the United States Embassy
Monuments of man and his sin
Heightening my empathy

White blocks representing Jews
Who were murdered
Because they held different views
Killed as ordered

They were taken together
Transported away
It did not matter the weather
Or if they had sway

They were demonized
By one leader
Terribly despised
Leading as a weeder

Eliminating the wretched
According to his beliefs
The population consented
The masses following their chiefs

Some tried to stop it
But they were taken too
They were in the bottom of a pit
And the rest knew

Go along or share their fate
The mass killings went on
Millions killed it was too late
They were all gone

How terrifying and awful
To comprehend and understand
How inhuman and unlawful
A horrible blight on their land

There have been other genocides
Through the ages
What corrupts us and divides
As we look through the history pages

Power and greed
Better than others
Do we not all bleed
As brothers and mothers

We must remember
This unspeakable sadness
We are all a witness and member
To this horrific madness

Soviet Military Monument

March 10, 2019, in Germany, Soviet War Memorial

The Soviet Union military monument right in downtown Berlin. There are 2,500 Soviet Union soldiers buried there.

I am surprised that this monument is still in the city.

Poem Soviet Union

> Memorial to fallen soldiers
> Including the Russians
> They carried us on their shoulders

Which can cause a lot of discussions

An evil communist nation
Killing their populace in the millions
What a great frustration
How they treated their civilians

Oppression
Subjugation
Starvation
Slavery

They had an iron grip
But we need their assistance
Anything but a courtship
For western culture existence

Europe was lost
Japan taking the far east
Jews experiencing the holocaust
We were facing the beast

The Soviet Union had the same enemies
And it was through a mutual need
We would seek our remedies
To finish and end this deed

The Soviet Union played their part
Helping to defeat the Japanese and Germans
So I guess we were all smart
But we did hear the sermons

They will be our foe
To fight in the future
A menace that would grow
Until we changed their ruler

After a long time past
The Soviet Union did crumble
Their country and allies trashed

After a global rumble

They are still here
As the Russian Federations
With a smaller sphere
And without admiration

So why keep their memorial
To honor their lost
We do not need a pictorial or tutorial
To remember how much it has cost

First Weather Issue - Cancelled Train

March 10, 2019, in Germany, Berlin Hauptbahnhof

I have to take a regular train at midnight and make two changes. I will get to Zurich 2 hours later than planned. Go with the flow.

I fixed my problem. Found train to Frankfort right now. A train in Frankfort that I will have 40 minutes to catch to Zurich. Get to Zurich by eight. No one can do it better than yourself.

Note to doctor: This does not bother me—this type of stress.

Berlin's Summary

I did not appreciate Berlin it seemed cold and unromantic. I was not inspired by its beauty. I was inspired by its history and by its memories to the Jews, Cold War, and Soviet Union. There is a tremendous amount of history in Berlin.

I think it is a must see city because of its historical significance.

Day 8 Zurich

Snow – Sleeping Car Cancelled

March 11, 2019, in Germany, Rottenmünster
Cold and snow falling on my way to Zunich, and I had a sleeper car canceled which made sleep much harder..

Advise 22 - Be Flexible

Something is going to go wrong no matter how hard you plan. My night train was cancelled due to the snow. I had to think quick and rearrange my route to get around the snow and to stay somewhat on track. I had to take two trains to get to my next stop but there was no sleeping car. I had planned to sleep but it is very difficult sitting in a second class train seat. I had to be flexible to get to my next stop and it was my only choice. I had no place to stay but on the trains.

I laid on two or three seats because no one was in the compartment with me. I woke up a few hours later and there were three people sitting across from me and another coming into the compartment to grab one of the seats I was lying on. How embarrassing. Be flexible.

Poem Girl on the Train

There she was
On the train
To my applause
What a strain

Strain of travel
Strain of boredom
Strain of loveless
Strain of loneliness

I admired her looks
She was all alone

Right out of a songbook
I was petrified as a stone

Do I talk to her
Or introduce myself
It was all a blur
A beautiful woman or enchanted elf

I do not know
I was so tired
She did glow
And one to be desired

But where does it go
I wrote her a poem
Events were moving slow
So much ho hum

My phone was dead
So I wrote it on paper
Admiration I said
And it was vapor

I do not remember
What I wrote
But I felt an ember
I wrote in the note

I never talked to her
Giving her my admiration
But it was a blur
With much frustration

I had to rush
To find my next train
I forgot my crush
Because I felt the drain

Tired
Worn out

Exhausted
Spent

She took my token
Of her great beauty
Leaving so much unspoken
She was a cutie

But I had to move on
And catch a train
She was gone
There was nothing to gain

She left the station
And I got on my ride
There was no flirtation
And gone was my pride

Why did I not talk
Or try harder
Was I in shock
Or just a martyr

Or reasonable
And understanding
This was not feasible
Or heading for a good landing

Zurich

The train station is right in the old section of Zurich. It was very convenient to the trolleys, restaurants, and shops on Bahnhofstrasse. This is Zurich main street through town and it had a nice trolley system which reduced my walking tremendously.

I do not know much about Zurich. Zurich is the largest city in Switzerland, and it is located in the north-central part of the country, on the shores of Lake Zurich. The city is known for its picturesque old town area, with its medieval architecture and narrow and winding streets. Zurich is a major financial hub if you watch any movies. Every goes to Zurich to get money or hide money. There are many museums in Zurich. This is one reason it is a popular tourist destination, offering a wide range of activities, including hiking in the nearby Swiss Alps, shopping in the high-end boutiques, and dining in the many restaurants. Additionally, Zurich is known for its high quality of life and is frequently ranked as one of the most livable cities in the world.

I enjoyed wandering the city and it was easy starting from the train station and jumping on a trolley.

Advice 23 - Make Copies of Passport

When you cross into Switzerland, they will take your passport. The conductor will return your passport but make a copy of your passport just in case. It is unnerving not to have your passport in your possession, but a copy will give you some comfort.

Zurich Train Station

March 11, 2019, in Switzerland, Zurich Main Station This is a village on to itself, laundries, two bookstores, toy store, restaurants, clothing shops, pharmacy, office supplies, tourist information, all trains, buses, and trams end up here.

Old Zurich

March 11, 2019, in Switzerland, Zurich Main Station Old Zurich

Zurich is very beautiful and picturesque.

The Alps in the Distance
March 11, 2019, in Switzerland, Zurich Main Station

Look for snow in the background because the northern part of the Alps begins near here.

Fickle Weather

March 11, 2019, in Switzerland, Zurich Main Station

The weather was funny. It changed from snow to sunny several times. At one time it was a regular blizzard.

Zurich Harbor

March 11, 2019, in Switzerland, Zurich Main Station

I like water no matter where it is or how big it is. Zurich Lake is no exception. The water is gorgeous with the clouds and mountain peaks in the distance. A small sailboat moving about the lake would be quite fun in the summer.

Advice 24 – Bring Good Walking Shoes

I planned to ride a bicycle mostly, so I did not have to walk as much, but Zurich was the exception. I walked everywhere for hours. I did not have walking shoes but boots. In hind sight, I wish I had brought one pair of walking shoes, but I did not think I had space for them – very foolish.

Zurich Churches

March 11, 2019, in Switzerland, Zurich Main Station

There were many churches in Zurich. So many churches there is a self-guided walking tour. The churches date between 500 and 1000 years ago.

Zurich was another city prominent in the Protestant Reformation and it is interesting the changes they made to how the worshipped God.

Zurich's Summary

I do not know what to think of Zurich. Zurich is part of Switzerland which is a neutral nation, and it has been for a long time. Zurich is home to the Protestant Reformation lead by Huldrych Zwingli. Zurich is a banking center of the world.

It has a beautiful old town along the river, Limmat with wonderful views of Lake Zurich and the alps.

I do not know what to say about this city, but it needs more investigating if I want to visit again especially the reformation church history.

Day 9 Budapest

Budapest

Budapest is the capital and largest city of Hungary. It is located in the northwest of the country, on the banks of the Danube River. It is known for its rich history, cultural heritage, and stunning architecture.

I wanted to go to Budapest because I had read that it was one of the most beautiful cities to visit and I was not disappointed on this leg of my trip.

Budapest Train Station

March 12, 2019, in Hungary, Budapest-Nyugati Pályaudvar

My first thoughts were scary because it was so run down. Dirty and not well maintained. The building is beautiful but falling apart.

I ran into a gyspy lady in the terminal and the scam she put on me was funny.

Poem - Gypsy

I always placed my bag
Into a train station locker
My bag was hard to haul and drag
It was heavy as a footlocker

I went to the locker area
And put in the token
And what a shocker
It would not open

I tried and tried
But to no avail
I needed a guide
And here is my tale

A little old lady

Came to my assistance
I did not think it was shady
I gave no resistance

She took my money
And made the locker work
How funny
I gave her a tip with a smirk

I went to the train office
To tell them there was an issue
And they said to be cautious
She is one of the unrighteous

What
What did that mean
They thought I was a nut
Was she a witch or unclean

A gypsy
Scamming you
Was I tipsy
But they knew

She jammed the machine
So it did not operate
Wandering upon the scene
Hoping you took the bait

She wanted the tip
The little extra I gave her
First time on this trip
Taken like an amateur

How remarkable
This little story
Right out of an amusement carnival
Or nursery rhyme allegory

Outside there were street vendors and taxi drivers scrambling for business.

Rough to Good

The further that I walked from the train station toward the river it all changes. The streets are cleaner and prettier and there are more shops and restaurants. Pretty streets and shops. You can tell that you are moving from a poorer section of town to a richer section. I ventured toward the main tourist area or Váci utca and the New Main Street. I knew if I got to the river, I would find everything to see.

Advice 25 – Patience

I learned to be more patient in these cities especially when I first got off the train. Most of the rail stations are in the older parts of the city where it seems to be poorer and more run down. This is the first thing that I saw, and it gave me a false impression of the city. Remain patient and do not judge until the end.

March 12, 2019, in Hungary, Vörösmarty tér

Budapest on the River

March 12, 2019, in Hungary, Vörösmarty tér

The main attractions are on the river. There is a tremendous amount of activity along the river.

Starbucks is the New Travel Center.

March 12, 2019, in Hungary, Vörösmarty tér

During my travels, I found Starbucks to be the best travel center. You can get a good cup of coffee, Americano for me and the food is trustworthy. Starbucks had power outlets to charge your phone or tablets, excellent wi-fi, and spotless bathrooms.

If I was in advertising, I would pitch a commercial for Starbucks to promote their establishments as travel centers in Europe. In every major city, I could depend upon Starbucks for consistent and reliable service.

The view from the Budapest Starbucks was fantastic. I sat outside in the sun and took in the sights up and down the river.

Advice 26 – Free Wi-Fi

The best place to get free wi-fi is Starbucks. You can depend upon charging you phone at a Starbucks. A second great place is the city libraries.

Views from Starbucks.

West Tennessee

March 12, 2019, in Hungary, Vörösmarty tér

When I left Budapest, traveling west looked like West Tennessee. Maybe it was the flatness and farmland, but I got the feeling I was traveling through the countryside in Tennessee.

Budapest's Summary

What a shocker! This is a gorgeous city along the Danube River with palaces, and blocks and blocks of beautiful buildings. The cost of visiting is very low compared to the rest of Europe – very good bargain.

There is a great deal of history with the Romans, Mongols, Czarist Russia, Ottoman, World War I Allied powers, and Soviet Union occupying and submitting the city to their laws. Also, Budapest was known as Jewpest with twenty-five percent of its population Jewish There are many stories of individuals in World War II saving many Jews from the Germans.

There are many places still to explore including Turkish bath houses and islands in the Danube River. I need one to two weeks in this city to explore and this city is on my list to return to in the near future. The top of my list

Prayer Budapest

Dear Father,

Thank you for this stop. I enjoyed myself, and I am thankful for the opportunity to travel Europe. You are magnificent and all powerful. Thank you for blessing me.

In Jesus name I pray

Amen

Day 10 Warsaw

Warsaw

Warsaw is the capital and largest city of Poland. It is located on the Vistula River in east-central Poland. This is a city rich in history. Warsaw has been conquered, destroyed, and rebuilt many times.

I put this city on my tour because of its fortitude to keep surviving and striving.

Warsaw Train Station

March 13, 2019, in Poland, Czyste

The train station was excellent—four stories of shops, restaurants, and stores. Next store was a three-story mall full of shops and stores that we know. Poland's currency to the dollar is cheap. Flowers are 40 cents, small bag groceries are 3.00 dollars, museum rates are $4.00 to enter. A very inexpensive city and so was Budapest.

Stroll to Warsaw Old City

Advice 27 – Get Lost

I got lost walking from the train station to the old city of Warsaw. I was surprised at the things that I got to see while lost. I saw beautiful monuments off the beaten track and beautiful buildings in many different architectural styles. If you get lost, then look for the good and the unexpected in each city.

March 13, 2019, in Poland, Towarzystwo Warszawskie Przyjaciół Nauk

I strolled to the old city, passing new skyscrapers, a couple of parks, and a few churches. I enjoy walking because I get to see so many unique things which I would surely miss in a taxi or on a bus or the subway. I stayed close to the Royal Route linking the old city and the new city.

Warsaw Old Town

March 13, 2019, in Poland, Zygmunt's Column

The old town is lovely but none of it survived during WWII. The ancient city was flattened, and they rebuilt it to look very similar.

Old City Wall

March 13, 2019, in Poland, Warsaw Old Town Market Square

Warsaw Ghetto

March 13, 2019, in Poland, Nowe Miasto

There were two Warsaw ghettos not one.. A large one and a small one connected by a wooden bridge. All the Jews were crowded into the ghettos. For food supply, you had to work or no food. The work was for German war efforts like fixing shoes and clothing.

When the Warsaw uprising occurred, it coordinated with the Soviet Union thinking they would come to liberate Warsaw. They did not.

This resulted in the Nazi Germans slaughtering the Polish resistance fighters.

Advice 28 – Say Yes

I took a taxi from the old city of Warsaw to the ghetto portion of Warsaw. My taxi driver said he would haul me around the ghetto neighborhood for ten dollars. I was leery of this guy because he asked me too many questions about where I was staying and who I was with etc, etc. Also, I felt he was trying to pick me up wanting to know if we could get dinner together and he would take me to the train station. A bit unusual, but I said yes to him giving me a tour of the ghetto area but no to the rest. He took me to the ghetto going down back alleys and showing me the old ghetto walls and explain ways the kids got in and out of the ghetto smuggling supplies in and out. It was a great tour.

You have to say yes sometime to see sights that are not part of the usual tours.

Warsaw, before WWII, was a Home to the Jews

March 13, 2019, in Poland, Nowe Miasto

I did not know that Poland was home to the majority of the Jewish population. They came to Poland because it treated them fairly, declaring laws for hundreds of years that Jews would be treated like every other citizen. The Jews prospered, and their population grew tremendously. Of course, that changed when Nazis marched into Poland. Three million Polish Jews were killed out of the six million Jews killed by Hitler. Most of the concentration camps were in Poland because that was where the majority of the Jews were located.

This is one of the saddest parts of history and it is memorable.

Poem Immigration or Migration

Migration to one
Is immigration to another
People we should not shun
Or smother

Populations have shifted
From nation to nation
And most have been gifted
As a result of their immigration

Nations have been rejuvenated
By this migration
But this is much debated
And caused much frustration

But look at the facts
The nations revived
And these peoples impacts
After they have arrived

Great migrations through the ages
Sending populations to other continents
It is written in history pages
Of its frequency and commonness

Jewish migration
Communist migration
Asian migration
European migration

Famine migration
Religious migration
Prosperity migration
Independence migration

Our own history
Shows of this process
And it is no mystery
That it can cause stress

They cannot come undocumented
Or without some basic requisites
Their arrival must be complemented
And here are the elements

Know the language
Know the civics
Know the customs
Know a skill

Do not come for free handouts
Or on your own
This will cause many doubts
And many will groan

Build a program
Educational and housing shelters
A buffer or dam
Sort of like smelters

Where change occurs
Making them better
This may take years
But better than a debtor

Owing us everything
Unwilling to pay
Only able to cling
To our government pay

Complaining is easy
Change is hard
I get queasy
By a process so marred

Change it now
Congress do your best
Show us you know how
And allow our country to be blessed

"Blessed be the Lord of the Universe, who motivated me to establish a study hall ... I shall bring to it ... 400 choice books".

David ben Menashe Darshan.
Shir hama'alot le-David (David's song of ascents), 1571

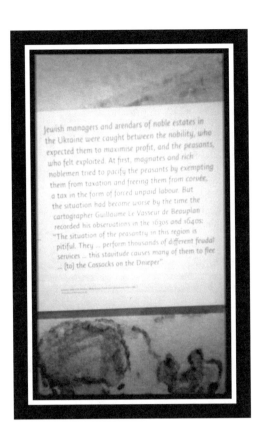

Jewish managers and arendars of noble estates in the Ukraine were caught between the nobility, who expected them to maximise profit, and the peasants, who felt exploited. At first, magnates and rich noblemen tried to pacify the peasants by exempting them from taxation and freeing them from corvée, a tax in the form of forced unpaid labour. But the situation had become worse by the time the cartographer Guillaume Le Vasseur de Beauplan recorded his observations in the 1630s and 1640s: "The situation of the peasantry in this region is pitiful. They ... perform thousands of different feudal services ... this stavitude causes many of them to flee ... [to] the Cossacks on the Dnieper."

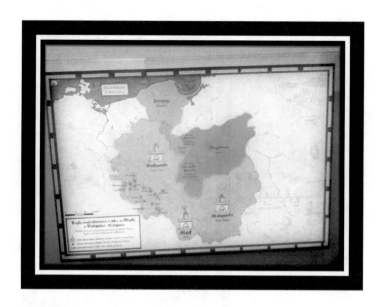

Poland Resistance - Printing Press

March 13, 2019, in Poland, Muzeum Powstania Warszawskiego

The printing press pictured was used in WWII by Jews to send out news. But even more impressive, the Polish resistance used it to fight against the occupation by the Soviet Union.

Poem Resistance

How do you get so brave
To fight evil

Not succumbing to the wave
Of ruin and upheaval

The odds are against you
There is no hope
For only a few
To fight on thin rope

They have the guns
And the organization
Killing your daughters and sons
Destroying your nation

What makes you think
That you can make a difference
Or become a kink
To the enemies interests

Pride
Stubbornness
Fortitude
Chivalry

I do not know
But it sounds like integrity
Maybe someone not going with the flow
Not accepting bestially

But whatever it is
You have to admire
And can I do this
If I had to face the hellfire

Young Fought in the Warsaw Uprising

March 13, 2019, in Poland, Muzeum Powstania Warszawskiego

Children serviced in the Warsaw uprising. They used a program like Boy Scouts during the German occupation to teach young ones how to help as couriers or smugglers.

This young boy was killed who was wearing that shirt. Look at bullet holes. Sad.

Warsaw's Summary

I am memorized by Warsaw and the suffering it endured during World War II.

I did not understand that Poland was free of Jewish persecution for hundreds of years so the jews flocked to Warsaw and the surrounding areas. They were safe to practice their religion.

What horrors the Warsaw people endured in fighting back against the Germans during World War II. They were very brave.

Visiting, seeing, and learning about this part of Warsaw's history was worth the trip to Warsaw and a must see when you come t Europe.

Day 11 Vienna

Vienna

Vienna is a city with a rich history and culture that dates back to the Roman Empire. Vienna is a must see when you go to Europe. The city is known for its beauty and its music, but I think of it as a bastion to western and Christian civilization.

The Ottoman were turned back three times from conquering Vienna. If they would of conquered Vienna it would have been a gateway to the rest of Europe.

Also, Vienna is known for its coffee houses where people have sat down and talked about their philosophies from Stalin and Hitler to Freud

Vienna is one of the top five cities to visit and explore. I used a bicycle for this city so I did not follow the main city street, Kärntner Straße. I was to venture out on bicycle trails to see more of the city.

Vienna Gigantic City - Bicycle It

March 14, 2019, in Austria, Neue Aula (Alte Universität)

The city is so spread out and there are so many large parks, bicycling was the best way to get around. Bicycle paths joined the parks to the rest of the city traveling along the Danube River.

Vienna Wandering

March 14, 2019, in Austria, Leopoldstadt

As I walked and rode my bicycle, there were little pockets of shops, hotels, and restaurants. Plenty of cool places to explore.

Advice 29 – Act Like a Tourist

In some cities, it is best to act like a tourist. People can be friendly and extremely helpful. I entered int more conversations when I asked about a monument or asked how to get to a tourist location. Most of the time, I said I am tourist and I am lost can you help me. I think it did help me.

Shopping Area - Naschmarkt

March 14, 2019, in Austria, Vienna University of Technology

This is the gigantic shopping and market area. One mile-long easily. It reminded me of Lincoln Road in Miami Beach but classier. Maybe more like Miracle Mile in Chicago..

Vienna Large River (Danube)

March 14, 2019, in Austria, Wien Donaukaibahnhof

The Danube goes through the city with bicycle and walking paths. It is a very nice ride. This river goes through Budapest too. The part that looks like a ditch is called the little river.

Advice 30 – Portable Power Bank Charger

I found using my cellphone all day for travel directions and pictures it would drain the battery down near empty. If I was staying in a hotel, it was no problem to plug my cellphone in to wall socket and recharge it. But, when you are moving from city to city on a train there is nowhere to charge your cellphone.. It is a problem.

A portable power bank charger or two is a necessary to keep your cellphone charged for directions or entertainment.

Vienna's Summary

An eloquent city to visit with miles of beautiful lanes and parks. Many bicycle trails, too.

Vienna stopped the Ottoman twice from conquering their city and spreading into Europe in the 16th and 17th centuries. An impressive accomplishment.

There are ghosts of composers to dictators and socialist rummaging around the city. The composers calling Vienna home were Wolfgang Amadeus Mozart, Joseph Haydn, Ludwig van Beethoven, and Johannes Brahms. The local coffee houses had Adolf Hitler, Leon Trotsky, Josip Broz Tito, and Joseph Stalin all living here in 1913 just a few miles from each other. Also throw in Sigmund Freud in that year, too.

Vienna is a city of influencers, and it is a great city to make you think about life and the world. I want to revisit it and experience more of it history and culture.

Miles of Vineyards

March 15, 2019, in Italy, Rivoltella

Miles and miles of vineyards in the countryside on the way to Milan. A wine tour would be exciting.

.

Day 12 Milan

Milan

Milan was a convenient place to start and stop traveling through Europe. Maybe, that is why it is an important city to visit in Europe. Milan is the gateway to Italy form the north, the Spaniards conquered it once before, Venice and Florence used it during their reins of power, and it is a great financial and innovative center in Italy and Europe today.

I do not know if I would have come here if it was a convenient place to stop on my tours, but I am glad I did. It may be the future of Europe.

Advice 31 – Read A History Book

I knew nothing about Milan. Next time, I will read a history book about Milan. When you know more about places you are visiting it makes it much more exciting and rememberable.

I did read about Thessalonica, so I remember more form that visit then I do in Milan. Also, I know the books of the New Testament, Acts, Corinthians, and Thessalonians and when I visited those cities it was relevant to my knowledge.

Read about the cities before you go.

Wandering Milan

March 15, 2019, in Italy, Milano Centrale Railway Station

 Just wandering or lost whichever. I left the train station and headed toward the Duomo which was the number one thing to see on my list.

Milan Wandering Part 2

March 15, 2019, in Italy, Milano Centrale Railway Station

More wandering

Public Parks

March 15, 2019, in Italy, Giardini pubblici Indro Montanelli build this park 1800's for rich and aristocracy. Now it can be used by anyone.

Duomo Cathedral - Wow!

March 15, 2019, in Italy, Museo del Duomo

A beautiful church! There is a painting inside of the last supper. There is a big rally in Duomo Plaza. The kids are marching are against the government and its stand on a green environment. There were thousands and thousands of people.

Prayer Duomo

Dear Creator,

Thank you for Duomo. It is a beautiful church constructed to honor and glorify you. Thank you for the opportunity to see this church. It is so gloriousd like you Lord.

In Jesus name I pray

Amen

Milan Castle

March 15, 2019, in Italy, Arena Civica

A gigantic castle

Advice 32 – Eat the Street Food

There were food vendors around the castle and many people were flocking to these food vendors. I decided to get something to eat from one of the food carts. The food was hot and delicious. I got a good portion of food, and the price was very reasonable. It made a great picnic looking at the massive walls on a bright sunny day.

THE CASTLE AS A MILITARY FORTRESS

Throughout its long and complex history, the Castle has always played an important military role. At the end of the 15th century, in fact, the structure resembled a barricaded enclosure, encircled by a moat, which was connected to the city walls by fortified gatehouses (rivellini) with drawbridges and defended by a curtain wall called the Ghirlanda facing the countryside. A covered walkway was tunnelled through the counterscarp of the moat. It ran along the entire length of the outer perimeter, had a barrel-vaulted ceiling and was lit by slit-like openings. This subterranean passageway, in which artillery posts can still be seen today, also opened into others. The walls of the Sforza enclosure, five metres thick in places and with their foundations at the bottom of the moat, rose up obliquely as an escarpment to redondone. From there, they rose vertically up to the ramparts. With foreign domination from the 16th century onwards, the Castle became an exclusively military site and was used as a barracks for all the various troops. New kinds of artillery and new strategic needs occasioned different modifications to the Castle, such as the lowering of the round towers and the construction of a fortified gatehouse and barbican (rivellino) in front of the principal entrance, effectively altering its original appearance. The most important period of transformation was that of the Spanish occupation (1535-1706), when a revolution in fortified structures gave rise to the so-called "bastion-style" architecture. With the construction of two fortified earthworks called tenaglie (pincers, due to their overall shape) the Castle was connected to the new defensive walls of the city projected by Gianmaria Olgiati, a military engineer in the service of the dukedom of Milan – from 1541 onwards. Between 1560 and 1600 another external wall was added to the Castle – a massive system of defence in the shape of a six-pointed star with a bastion at each point. Halfway through the 17th century, new reinforcements called "half moons" were added, connecting the points of the stars, since, by then, the structure was considered insufficient.

The powerful, bastioned citadel, pictured faithfully in numerous contemporary prints continued to function efficiently even during the Austrian domination (1706-1796) until the demolition decree issued on 23rd June 1800 by Napoleon Bonaparte. Napoleon had the Spanish bastions removed from around the Castle in order to create a new public area – the future Foro Bonaparte – and thereby returned the Castle, albeit in poor condition, to the city.

The Milanese fortress, newly occupied by the Austrians from 1831 to 1859, was once again used as a war machine during the Cinque Giornate (the five days of uprising, 18-22 March 1848) of Milan, when General Radetzky installed his artillery on top of the round towers in order to fire on the citizens in revolt. The Castle became a barracks for the Italian troops after the Unification of Italy (1861) and finally was ceded to the city of Milan in 1887.

...nd Savoy forces. Engraving, 1734. Milan.

Milan Loves Dogs

March 15, 2019, in Italy, Giardini pubblici Indro Montanelli

The people of Milan love their dogs. They are on trains, subways, and everywhere. I wish The Keeper could see this and live here. One ran from his master went into the fountain soaking wet.

Gigantic Graveyard

March 15, 2019, in Italy, Museo delle Arti Decorative Or mausoleum.

Milan - It is Friday!

March 15, 2019, in Italy, Milano Centrale Railway Station

There were large crowds all over the train station. Friday, it is time to travel Europe.

Milan's Summary

Milan was surprising. I knew nothing about Milan just remembering finance and the fashion industries. I did not know the breath of its history or its composition with romantism and futuristic thinking.

Milan grew while the rest of Italy shrank. Milan became more powerful financially with industrialization and it became the hub of economic activity in Europe.

I do not know if it is a city that I will revisit, but its melting pot of ideas and innovation and its role as a hub to the rest of Europe is interesting.

Day 13 Paris

Paris

Well, you have to go to Paris while you are in Europe. London or Paris are the number one city to visit with London being a city of our forefathers in the United States and of stoic resistance and Paris being the city of our first ally to the United States and the city of romance.

I went to Paris to experience the Paris of romance. I was not disappointed it was phenomenal.

French Countryside
March 16, 2019, in France, Lézinnes

The French Countryside was green, and everything was growing.

Advice 33 – Carry Ear Plugs and Eye Mask

I have been traveling on night train cars where you share a room with four strangers. I have done that two or three times, but this time it was quite different. A lady came into our compartment with a baby. The baby was crying, and she said this was her bunk with the baby. I was so, so happy that I had my ear plugs and my eye mask. I jumped into my bunk and put on ear plugs and eye mask and went right to sleep. I could faintly hear the baby crying. Ear plugs and eye mask are a must on night trains – be warned!

I got off the train and transferred to the subway. I went right to my motel because I had to get some laundry done. While I waited for my laundry, I figured out where I wanted to go and what I wanted to see. The subway was my main mode of transportation for Paris.

Doing My Laundry

March 16, 2019, in France, Place des Vosges

It is not all fun! Doing my laundry first thing in Paris. I am in the Bastille neighborhood and, I found a laundry mat. It looks fantastic, except I could not figure out how to use the machines. A kind lady helped me through sign language because we did not speak each other's language. Where is that Google translator when I need it? It was only one-half mile from the hotel. Woo hoo!

Prayer Laundry Mat

Heavenly Father,

You are so gracious and true over the small things. I did not have a clue but you sent someone to help me and it was a blessing. Thank you Lord for the women who gave me instructions.

In Jesus name I pray

Amen

220

Advice 34 – City Attraction Cards

A good bargain to go into various attractions and sometimes to get discounts on transportation purchase a city discount card. The price of entry to a large number of museums and other attractions can be quite expensive but with you get a good discount purchasing a city discount card. A bonus is access to discounted public transportation such as subways and buses.

Arc de Triumph

March 16, 2019, in France, Arc De Triomphe

A fun trip here. The Yellow Vests were out in force protesting. I heard loud booms which I guess was tear gas. The authorities shut down the subways. Yes, this made my life extremely difficult. I had to improvise going miles out oif my way to get around Paris.

Colonel Birmingham - "Stay out of crowds."

March 16, 2019, in France, Arc De Triomphe

Anything can happen in a crowd is what my father told me all the time. Crowds can turn into a riot before you know. You will be caught in tear gas and violence. So stay out of crowds and beware. He always had these little sayings and moist of the time he was right.

Eiffel Tower

March 16, 2019, in France, Centre Sportif Emile Anthoine

The journey was one-half the fun. All the metro stations were shut down one mile from the tower. I had to get close and to walk.

Advice 35 – Keep Your Guard Up

In any city or crowded circumstances keep your guard up. I was leaving the subway on the way to the Eiffel Tower, and I was on a one person, very tight escalator. I noticed two you adults rushing up behind me pushing past people and there was nowhere for them to go because the escalator was full of people.

One of the young men bumped hard into me and pushed past me while the second guy tried to pick my wallet out of my back pocket. My wallet was not there so I was not worried, so I turned around and said excuse me with a stare. They took off up the escalator pushing their way through the crowd.

Keep your guard up these things happen all over the world.

River Seine

March 16, 2019, in France, Pont au Change

Views of River Seine

227

Excitement

March 16, 2019, in France, Collégiale Saint-Honoré

Police vehicles rushing about. Each police car has 3 or 4 policemen inside. I figure this has to do with the Yellow Vests.

Louvre

March 16, 2019, in France, Jardin du Carrousel

I wandered through and around the Louvre. It was very crowed, and some entrances were closed. Usually there are nine to twelve entrances, so I did a lot of walking to get inside. It wore me out, but the view was worth it.

Cite - Notre De

March 17, 2019, in France, Île de la Cité

I walked to Notre De and sat outside at a restaurant to eat lunch in view of the cathedral. It started to spit snow, but it made the trip that more memorable. It was lovely. There was a little market, but it was no comparison to the Bastille Market.

Prayer Notre Da

Dear God,

Another church erected in your honor. This church is beautiful and reminder to all who see it how beautiful you are Lord. Thank you for allowing the Parisians to honor you with this church and may it stand forever like you Lord.

In Jesus Name I pray

Amen

The Cathedral of Notre De up close.

Day 14 Paris

Bastille Market - Unbelievable!!

March 17, 2019, in France, Place de la Bastille

A must see attraction in Paris. The market had vegetable, fruit, meat, fish, and merchandise stands. The fish stands have every kind of fish, ell, and oysters. It was very festive.

Do not expect to see the Bastille it was torn down a long time ago and actually it sits in the middle of the Bastille Market with four subway stops around it.

Paris More Wanderings

March 17, 2019, in France, Alexandre III Bridge

More wanderings in Paris

Advice 36 – Eat like the Locals

I went to subway early in the morning and I was hungry. I watched the locals go up to the food counter and they ordered an espresso and a loaf of bread. They drank the expresso like a shot downing it in one gulp and took off with their bread for breakfast.

I ordered the same thing just like a Parisian. It was fun watching the people and their local customs. I recommend watching what the locals are eating and drinking and partake. It will be a grand memory of your trip and you will not go wrong.

Paris' Summary

Paris is Paris. A beautiful city that has not changed in layout or structure in hundreds of years mainly through Government control of the zoning laws and it is one of the few capitals not destroyed by war. Napoleon and Napoleon III ensured Paris' beauty.

There are many places to visit from monuments to museums. The churches and palaces are easy to visit and admire.

Paris is known as the City of Light or the City of Art where great movements of enlightenment in arts and politics has taken place with the greatest advancements in the nineteenth and twentieth centuries. Paris is a city of inspiration.

The city has a gigantic Muslim and Jewish population which increases its diversity.

I like Paris and I plan to return but I think it is expensive and crowded but you cannot beat the feeling of romantism while you wander there.

More Alps

March 18, 2019, in Italy, Masano
Northern Italy

Day 15 Florence

Florence

During the Renaissance, Florence was a rich and powerful city it led the world in thinking and financing. The great artist and thinkers Leonardo da Vinci and Michelangelo both worked and lived here. Machiavelli wrote his book the Prince, here. The family of Medici who lived here, ruled the financial world financing these artists and the rest of Europe including the Popes and kings and queens of many nations. They made and broke kingdoms. Two of the Medici family would become Popes.

Florence was the city of humanism thinking and the development of the Renaissance ideals of art, science, and culture.

Florence is a city rich in history and culture and is a popular tourist destination known for its art, architecture, and beautiful landscapes. Look at the section on overview. The view is breath taking.

This is a city to visit and appreciate. Today it is just a city form history, but it created and expanded many of the great ideas of western civilization.

Skipping Venice for now

March 18, 2019, in Italy, Venezia Mestre Railway Station

There is rain and fog in Venice, so I am jumping to Florence. Once again the advantages of having a train pass. It cost me nothing to change my plans.

Florence - Wandering

I wandered from the train station to my hotel. I passed many of the sights that I wanted to see along the Via dei Calzaiuoli. The main street and shopping areas in Florence.

Advice 37 - Eat Main Meal for Lunch

I ate my main meal for lunch for a number of reasons and in Florence it was no difference. I had trouble meeting my landlord, so I stopped, and I ate lunch at a restaurant near my flat. I used the time to review what I was going to do next. The food was delicious, and they have a lower price for lunch just like most places in the world. I got a rest, I got reorganized, I waited for someone, and I saved money.

March 18, 2019, in Italy, Uffizi Gallery
Wandering

244

248

Florence Wandering 2

March 18, 2019, in Italy, Orsanmichele

Advice 38 – Universal Travel Adaptor

I had no problems with charging my cellphone in most cities but not in Florence. The wall outlets were old fashion, just like my flat. I had to skip charging my cellphone this night. Pack a universal travel adaptor for emergencies.

Overview Florence

March 18, 2019, in Italy, Piazzale Michelangelo

A grand view of Florence form the heights overlooking the city. I walked or hiked up the mountain and it was tiring but well worth the trip.

Florence needs three days to see shops, restaurants, museums, statues, and buildings.

Florence - Ponte Vecchino

March 18, 2019, in Italy, Pignone

The renown shops on the bridge. The shops were full of jewelry - diamonds, and gold.

Florence's Summary

Florence is beautiful especially from the mountain southeast of the city. I hiked over there, and it was a long way up many steps but well worth the effort. It is simply gorgeous.

Florence is the center of the Renaissance with wonderful museums to visit and statues by Michelangelo of Davinci. Really, there is so much art in such a small area this is one of the best cities to visit to appreciate the flow from religious art and humanistic art.

I would like to revisit this city for two or three days and spend more time in the museums.

Day 16 Rome

Rome

Rome is the capital and largest city of Italy. It is located in the central-western part of the country. Rome is a city steeped in history, with many ancient ruins and monuments that have been preserved for thousands of years. Rome started as small state expanding to a republic led by two counsels to a dictator and then to an empire. Rome became the most powerful empire in the world increasing its territories through conquest and colonization throughout Europe, the Middle East and Africa. Rome has left its essence on western civilization to this day.

This is why Rome as one of the top five probably the third most important city to visit.

Additionally, Rome is home to the Vatican City, the smallest country in the world and the spiritual center of the Catholic Church. A wonderful sight to visit and experience.

I wandered from historical site to historical sight after I got off the train in Rome. I wandered down the Via del Corso taking a few side trips here and there. I took a different route back to the train station and it did not have as many historical attractions but it was fun watching people.

Advice 39 – Be Respectful

I was at the train station at the end of the day, and I was going to take a train out of Rome a few miles to a smaller town just to experience Italy in a different way. I asked where the line was for the train and the train staff told me over there. I waited in line twenty to thirty minutes, and they told me I was in the wrong line and to go to that line. I went to that line and after I got to the counter, I missed my train. I asked to go to another town, and they said my ticket would not do that. I got mad and argued with the train staff asking for the manager. I looked like a stupid buffoon or an angry tourist. Probably like a spoiled American. I needed to be

256

more patient and respectful, it was no big deal. I learned my lesson.

Rome Castle St Angelo

March 19, 2019, in Italy, Castel Sant'Angelo

Rome Colosseum

March 19, 2019, in Italy, Colosseum

Rome Forum

March 19, 2019, in Italy, Musei Capitolini

Rome Pantheon

March 19, 2019, in Italy, Fontana del Pantheon

Rome St Peter's Cathedral

March 19, 2019, in Italy, Castel Sant'Angelo

Advice 40 – Early Bird

I learned a long time ago; you have to get up and to get moving before the crowds appear. This is true for shopping and for touring. I think it was truer in Rome. I moved from one part of the city early in the morning without much difficulty but as the day wore on there were more and more people. The tourist attractions were more and more crowded along with the sidewalks. This is a truism – you have to be the early bird.

Rome's Summary

You have to go to Rome just because of the history of the Roman Empire and the Catholic Church. It is considered the center of western civilization and the Christian religion.

Rome is part of the Renaissance and Neoclassical movements. There are many museums, buildings, and statues to explore throughout Rome. The Popes for hundreds of years have supported these movements ensuring Rome would be one of the most beautiful cities in the world. The Vatican is priceless in visiting and touring its grounds.

Rome needs a good week to appreciate all that it has to offer.

Venice

Venice is a city in northeastern Italy, and it is situated on a group of 118 small islands that are separated by canals and linked by bridges. Venice is not as old as most European cities it was founded in the fifth century. The barbarians were attacking Rome and refuges started the city on these islands as refuge.

Venice grew as their maritime powers grew. They became a great naval power with ships powered by oars trading throughout the Mediterranean. Through their maritime commerce, they became a rich and powerful nation.

Their riches provided financing for the arts and ultimate power for Venice. Their power lasted until Portugal, Spain, Netherlands, and England created new trade routes to the world bypassing the Venice established trade routes in the Mediterranean.

Venice's lagoon and canals along with its unique architecture makes it picturesque and one of the most beautiful cities in Europe. I wandered from the train station along the canals to Piazza San Marco. There were plenty of shops and restaurants along the way.

Advice 41 - Open Mind

I was in almost a panic mode because there must of be thousands of kids all over the place. The streets were packed with teenagers, and it made me uncomfortable. The crowds were so tight, and it was hard to get around. I do not like crowds and pushy ones at that, so a bunch of teenagers are the pushiest. I buckled down and I kept an open mind. They are not here to harm anyone, they are here for a Eurozone event. I think it was something to do with the environment but never the less, I remembered why I was there. To tour the city just like these kids..

Venice - St Mark's Cathedral

March 19, 2019, in Italy, St Mark's Basilica

Venice Grand Canal

March 19, 2019, in Italy, Cpo Santa Margherita Melody Hudson

Fabulous!

Venice Shopping & Canals
March 19, 2019, in Italy, Canal Grande

Venice's Summary

Venice is beautiful but amaze to navigate with all of the canals and bridges. I walked from the train station to the Grand Canal, and it was splendid. I toured many back alleys and little pedestrian bridges. I saw more ordinary Venetians and what they were doing. It made the trip fabulous.

You have to ride a gondola and tour the canals on a water taxi. The architecture is a memory to envision.

There are many tourists and it can be extremely crowded, so I do not know if it will ever be a future stop.

Day 17 Alps

Alps

Weird Rock Formations and Plenty of Vineyards

March 20, 2019, in Italy, Laghetti

Poem - Vineyards

Lines and lines
Vineyards everywhere
Making wonderful wines
Passed on from heir to heir

Pinot Bianco
Pinot Grigio
Gewurztraminer
Shaiva

For generations
The alps are full of grapes
Coming from many nations
Dotting the landscape

Italy
Germany
France
Austria

They are high acid whites
Or lighter bodied reds
Grown on these heights
With very common threads

From high altitude regions
With cool climates
For these reasons
You will not find much dryness

Sweet for a picnic
Light for salads
Not a tremendous kick
But made by the gallons

Unique flavors
Pleasant to the taste
They can be lifesavers
So sip with no haste

Wandering Alps

March 20, 2019, in Austria

Vineyards on the mountainside

March 20, 2019, in Italy, Klausen

Hanging Out Here!

March 20, 2019, in Italy, Cattedrale Metropolitana di San Pietro

No running this afternoon. I took a rest period on the train. Late train that is wandering around the Alps and tomorrow to Bari to catch the ferry to Greece.

Poem Alps

How majestic
And glorious
Now very domestic
Not as notorious

In its day
Hard to pass
A terrible fray
With snow in mass

Armies crossed at times
Hunters and gathers
But that was a long time
When the snow scatters

Today new road and tunnels
Make easier to transgress
With less struggles
And less stress

But the beauty is still there
Mountains and passes
Way up in the air
Enjoyment for the masses

Tourism is its big thing
Alpinism
On s holiday fling
Strong sense of naturalism

Strong forces in the mountains
Hiding in the valleys and peaks
Or wherever the encounters
Romanticism leaks

An enduring feeling
Of easiness and bliss
Maybe a sense of healing
Or a warm kiss

The snow covered mountain tops
And the pretty valleys
Along with scattered rocks
And tight sunlit alleys

Dotted with cattle
And grapevines
So do not tattle
Or publish headlines

It is still charming
And untainted
Too many maybe harming
So keep them unacquainted

Day 18 Bari

Bari

Bari was a surprise. I went here to catch a ferry to Greece. I did not think anything of Bari being a place to visit but it definitely was a fine addition to my tour.

Bari sits on the water and is a large port. They have an old walled city with houses and alley ways intermixed in the walls and the city. It was exciting to venture upon the walls and to explore the city of Bari.

I wandered along the walls until I got to the Piazza Mercantile which is the usual town square with shops and coffee houses. I like this routine and tradition. Go to the center of town and observe.

I found beautiful views of the sea and I was entertained by the maritime life here.

I enjoyed a wonderful seafood meal at one of the local restaurants.

This was an extraordinary stop and I want to come back and visit.

More Port Bari –
Water and Boats March 21, 2019, in Italy, Mercato del Pesce

An Excellent Way to Start the Day!

March 21, 2019, in Italy, Giardini di Piazza Cesare Battisti Palm trees

Bari Wandering
March 21, 2019, in Italy, Piazza Garibaldi

Advice 42 - Try New Food

I was in Bari, and I follow my own advice to eat my main meal at lunch so I can get reorganized and prepared for the rest of the day. I found a restaurant near the docks; I asked them to give me the best local food that they had available. It was seafood and it was fabulous. I did not ask what I was eating but I think it was octopus, and sea urchins. The best way to try new food is t ask for their local foods and eat it without complaint.

Lawn Control

March 21, 2019, Adriatic Sea

The locals had placed a donkey in a traffic square to eat the grass - lawn control.

Castello Normanno Svevo

March 21, 2019, in Italy, Bari Ferry Port

A grand fort with thick, huge walls was guarding the Port of Bari.

Wow - fish, squid, oysters - fresh!

March 21, 2019, in Italy, Giardino san Filippo Smaldone

These fishermen caught their catch and were selling it at the docks. They were selling fish, oysters, shrimp, sea urchins, and squid. They were standing around and others were drinking beer and playing cards. My kind of place.

Bari - Port Adriatic Sea

March 21, 2019, in Italy, Porto Vecchio

City Wall - Walking, Bicycles, Houses

March 21, 2019, in Italy, Giardino Croce Rossa Italiana

More Port Bari

March 21, 2019, in Italy, Porto Vecchio

Advice 43 – Download Google Translate

In most of Europe, I found people spoke English or some type of broken English. It was not until I ventured into southern Italy, which is probably not a high tourist location for English speaking peoples that I seemed to have a greater language barrier. Google translate would have been very handy here in Bari.

I was unable to communicate with most of the local populace. I think the country of Italy was the hardest to communicate with in Europe. I had an easier time in Russia speaking to the Russians then the Italians.

Remember to download Google translate to make life easier.

Inside City Walls

March 21, 2019, in Italy, Bari

The walls were honeycombed with tiny alleyways with apartments, shops, groceries, and cafes. Lots of older people in 70's and 80's. Small vehicles would not get through the alleys and turns. It was cool to wander through the alleys.

Bari Sailing Club

March 21, 2019, in Italy, Porto Vecchio

I talked to some guys at Bari Sailing Club. They had a few Lasers, Sunfish, and a few others. I think it is the one made for Navy Academy and is now used for racing, but I do not remember its name.

Bari - Roman Ruins

March 21, 2019, in Italy, Piazza Ferarese

I found a few Roman ruins which should not be surprising since I am in Italy.. The road is covered in two layers, and it was the foundation of the city wall—the other ruins were just columns in the old town.

Sundown Bari

March 21, 2019, in Greece, Karavostasi

Bari's Summary

A highlight of my trip and it was a great find. I traveled to Bari to get on a ferry to Greece, but what a surprise to find such a wonderful and romantic place.

Bari is a seaport in southern Italy with historical defensive walls surrounding the city. I explored up and down the walls walking along the Adriatic Sea. The seafood and maritime atmosphere was abundant.

I would love to come back to Bari and stay for a month. This was an awesome place to visit.

Prayer Bari

Dear Heavenly Father

Thank you for this wonderful city and its beauty. I am blessed to have seen it and experienced it. I give you all the thanks for allowing me to see so much of Europe.

In Jesus name I pray

Amen

Ferry Italy to Greece

March 21, 2019, Adriatic Sea

Ferry Italy to Greece.

There was no passengers. The ship was empty because it was their off-season. They say the ship is packed in summer with people sleep everywhere - floors, hallways, couches, etc. Look closely, you see one

guy on laying on the floor.

Moon over the Adriatic Sea

March 21, 2019, Adriatic Sea

Day 19 Greece

Greece

Greek Shoreline

March 22, 2019, Ionian Sea
Shoreline of Greece.

Patras Landing

March 22, 2019, in Greece, Liménas Patrón

I was waiting for the train to Athens and Thessaloniki. It took me a long time to find the train station and it was along walk to the transport bus. I should have hired a taxi if I knew it would be such an ordeal.

302

Tomorrow Apostle Paul's Travels

March 22, 2019, in Greece, Liménas Patrón

I am traveling to Thessalonica tonight. I want to go to Neapolis and Philippi and on the second day see Thessalonica and Berea. The third day I will travel to Athens and Corinth. This will be a great visit.

Prayer Apostle Paul's Trips

Dear Lord,

I am in awe of the opportunity that I have received to travel in Paul's footsteps and to see where he preached and lived. Thank you for this chance to match scripture with a geographic location. You are super to give me this season of my life.

In Jesus name I pray

Amen

Sundown Greece

March 22, 2019, in Greece, Liménas Patrón

Patras sundown.

304

Athens Train Center

March 22, 2019, in Greece, Athens Larisa Station

There was mass chaos for a Friday weekend. There were no seats available on the train and there were people everywhere. I got no pictures because it was too crazy. My only picture was the full moon.

One observation is that there is one police officer that I have seen in all other countries, but in Athens there are 5 to 10 police officers and/or soldiers with assault rifles. Two motorcycle cops just cruised up.

Day 20 Thessaloniki

Thessaloniki

Thessaloniki is a port city located in northern Greece, on the Thermaic Gulf of the Aegean Sea. It is the second-largest city in Greece.

The city has been ruled by many nations and empires over the past two thousand years. A diverse group of peoples have lived in Thessaloniki including Jews, Muslims, and Christians. This diversity has created many blends of food and experiences to enjoy.

Poem Thessalonica

A most wonderful place
Full of dreams
People with grace
A perfect place it seems

I enjoyed the sea
And its blue silkiness
Ships as far as you can see
Swimmers and rowers giddiness

Moving about
Left to right
And that was my route
From dawn to night

Jumping from one attraction
To the next
Always stopped by a distraction
Or lost perplexed

But this was my city
The best on the trip
Nothing compares or as pretty
To the people and fellowship

Paul taught about Christ
Gigantic market
Wonderful views
History traveled here

Roman ruins
Prayer rooms
Great food
Grand fortresses

Dog lovers
Hustle and bustle
Scenic parks
Alleys to explore

And on and on
So much to share
Resulting in a talking marathon
But it is not fair

You need to go
And find out in person
The fabulous city and its show
And make your own romantic version

Thessaloniki, My First Thought - Back in USSR

March 23, 2019, in Greece, Ágios Pávlos

I was very uneasy when I got off the train here. I felt like that I was back in the USSR - block apartments, graffiti, and trash. I traveled down the Egnatia Street.
After I got closer to the city center, it got better and better. I ran into the bay with 5 to 10 crews rowing and joggers.

And civilization - a travel center: Starbucks.

310

White Tower

March 23, 2019, in Greece, Ágios Pávlos

Thessaloniki Wandering

March 23, 2019, in Greece, pelókipoi

Advice 44 – Be Open to Strangers

I say hello and I smile to everyone that I pass on my travels..
I think it is basic kindness and courtesy.

On this trip while I was wandering Thessaloniki, I was
seeing the same women at all the tourist locations We were
walking to the same locations for miles. I finally said hi and
we chatted as we walked throughout the city. We spend the
next few hours touring Thessaloniki together. It was fun
having someone to talk to and to share the experience.

Take a chance and chat to strangers – say hello and smile.

Poem - Erika

Wow
So much power
And how
A beautiful flower

Growing and wandering
Around and around
Just pondering
Such a metropolitan town

Two people
Enjoying the time
So gleeful
Companions in rhyme

Sharing stories
Exploring the sights
And its glory
The ambiance excites

Ice cream delicious
The sunset warm and bright
It was auspicious
And just right

We chatted
Politics
The racial mix
And lit candlesticks

Economics
Finance
Graphic comics
And even France

So many discussions

Sharing our lives
No repercussions
It gave me hives

Erika's exciting bubbly self
Erika's sharp bright brown eyes
Erika's a classic on the bookshelf
Erika's sensibly wise

Erika was funny
Erika was smart
Erika was witty
Erika had a heart

She was unique
She was mysterious
She was sheik
She was nonserious

No doubt
I have a crush
And asked her out
Too much rush

But I knew
Steal a kiss
If it is true
But what a miss

She did not accept
And that is fine
I had overstepped
The fault is all mine

I will see her
Again and again
Not as a soft whisper
Or with disdain

But as a wonderful escape

As we took a stroll
In the beautiful landscape
Erika touched my soul

Thank you Erika
Secure in my thoughts
A gringo from America
Trying to connect lifes dots

But one thing is true
You will see me again
Brand new
In God's reign

Children of God
What a blessing
We will applaud
In heaven with no guessing

That will be
Our 2nd date
Totally totally free
How marvelous and great

My Office - Starbucks

March 23, 2019, in Greece, Ágios Pávlos

While sitting in Starbucks organizing my day, I look out at the Aegean Sea, ships, rowers, runners, and walkers. Very active.

Thessalonica Wandering 2
March 23, 2019, in Greece, Thessaloniki Ferry Port P

Thessalonica's Market is Gigantic

March 23, 2019, in Greece, Thessaloniki Ferry Port

Advice 45 – Haggle

In some countries it may be rude to ask for a lower price, but in many countries it is the custom. In Thessalonica's market, I would ask what your best price is or ask for twenty percent. Most of the time, we would get to ten percent.

There is a tremendous amount of fun in negotiating with the locals and many times it is expected of you.

Intercessory Prayer

March 23, 2019, in Greece, Sykiés

I was reading the book Life Together and Prayerbook of the Bible by Dietrich Bonhoeffer. He suggests intercessory prayer is essential in a healthy church. I noticed in Thessalonica the tiny prayer houses on the street near churches.

Prayer – Intercessory Prayer

Dear Might God,

I give thanks to you. I am reminded of why I should pray and why it is important. So many opportunities to present you with prayers in a formal setting is quite astonishing. I have seen nothing like it I Europe and I am thankful this opportunity. To you give all the glory.

In Jesus name I pray

Amen

It is convenient for individuals to stop and pray for people. I found it interesting the coincidence of reading it is essential, and seeing it made it easier to accomplish. Also, Erika was Catholic, and she encouraged me.

Advice 46 – Spontaneity

Take a chance. Do something new. Going into the prayer houses was new for me. I have not seen these in the United States, so it was a shock that the prayer houses were on every corner. When you act spontaneous it is exciting and rememberable.

Paul Preached and Talked to Disciples

March 23, 2019, in Greece, Ágios Pávlos
Monastery of Vlatadon

Poem Paul

An apostle
A man of courage
Spiritually colossal
One to encourage.

The New testament is full
Of his writings

More than a handful
And very exciting

To see his evangelism ways
And to understand and copy
Could lead you into a maze
And you could become sloppy

He gave it all
To be like Jesus
Did he have gall
Or did he know what frees us

I think it is God
And the Holy Spirit
So stand in awe
And get near it

Near it through reading
And praying
Plus conceding
And surveying

Your past deeds
And sins
Cleaning out the weeds
So you can change skins

Become a new person
It is promised
With this holy conversion
Become a psalmist

A composer of sacred songs
That do not have to be sung
To right earthly wrongs
For the elderly and young

Do good deeds
Preach the gospel

Plant the seeds
Join Gods hostel

A place of rest
A place to learn
A place to teach
A place to yearn

Yearn for God
And everlasting salvation
Be surprised and awed
At your new creation

Thessalonica Wandering 3

March 23, 2019, in Greece, Políchni

Byzantine Walls in Thessalonica

March 23, 2019, in Greece, pelókipoi
Ano Poli's Byzantine Walls,

Poem Byzantine Empire

The Byzantine civilization
Or Eastern Roman Empire
Lasted a long duration
But it ended in shellfire

How did it end
Why did it end
When did it end
Where did it end

Good questions
But this is not a history book
But here a few suggestions
So let us take a simplistic look

The empire was conquered by the Ottomans
The empire ended because of greed
The empire ended in roughly 1453
The empire ended with sacking of Constantinople

Simple but true
Greed ruins everything
Does not matter your worldview
It is the one thing

Money and more money
Power and more power
Not hilarious or funny
Corrupting and ready to devour

Man cannot help himself
He is bad to the bone
Take any history book off the shelf
And all national collapses are a clone

They are all the same
Eating away at the fabric of society
Pretty much the same old game
Without much variety

337

Thessalonica's Summary

I would like to live here. If I picked one place to live on my entire journey it would be Thessalonica. What a beautiful city with so much history. Its culture blends periods of occupation by Macedonians, Greeks, Romans, Byzantines, Venetians, Ottomans, and back to Greeks.

Thessalonica has a maritime importance, and it had the Roman road, Via Egnatia, running through it. This was a major thoroughfare to Asia and the Middle East.

The Apostle Paul lived here and preached as documented in the New Testament book, Thessalonians. The Christian communities Philippi, Berea, and Philippi are very close.

What else make Thessalonica interesting was the Young Turks formed here and overthrew the Ottoman Empire, and the Jews were the majority of the population for many hundreds of years. They immigrated from Spain, and it became a city for Jews. The Germans ended the Jewish city with a ghetto established for them and ninety percent transported to extermination camps.

There are many parks, museums, and monuments. There is the sea and national parks close by to Thessalonica.

I find the city to be fascinating and well worth exploring for an extended period of time.

Greeks are Very Patriotic - Flags

March 23, 2019, in Greece, Kallithéa

Greek national flags are up everywhere. Monday is a national holiday.

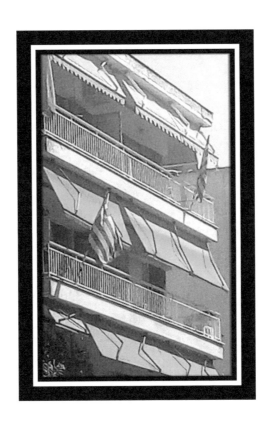

Day 22 Corinth

Corinth

Ancient Corinth was a wealthy and influential city in Greece, located on the Isthmus of Corinth Old Corinth was a major commercial center because ships were carried across the isthmus from one sea to another saving a week of travel. Corinth was a strategic city for this reason.

The old Corinth city was an important center for Christianity with Paul living here and teaching here. Paul picked cities with strategic important as a trade route to share the gospel.

Corinth was literally forgotten after Roman fell. The old city was abandoned, and it decayed into nothing.

The new Corinth was built alongside the old Corinth in the past 200 years.

Corinth is a short train ride from Athens, and I went there to see the city that I read about in the New Testament.

Back to Corinth Tonight

March 24, 2019, in Greece, fithea

I will check out old and new Corinth tomorrow.

Present Day Corinth

March 25, 2019, in Greece, Evangelístria

Ancient Corinth

March 25, 2019, in Greece, Peirene Fountain

Paul lived, preached, and worked in these ruins. Fabulous visit.

Corinth Canal and Ancient Corinth

March 25, 2019, in Greece, Corinth Canal

They moved ships across the isthmus on rollers before the canal was built.

346

Corinth's Summary

A city of Greek, Roman, and Christian historical significance not far from Athens.

This is a wonderful city to visit with its historical ruins littering the landscape..

A revisit is in order.

Athens

Athens is the capital and largest city of Greece. It is one of the world's oldest cities, with a history spanning over 3,400 years. Athens was the center of ancient Greek civilization and the birthplace of Western democracy.

To me it is one of the top five cities to visit maybe one the biggest reasons is the weather is perfect. Not too hot and not too cold.

I like Athens because it has been conquered many times with tremendous ups and downs, but it seems crawl back. Athens gets back up and becomes the center of world attention. A beautiful city.

I wandered out of the Ermou which is one of the touristy streets. It was a short walk to my hotel and that was my first stop.

Advice 47 – Join a Facebook Group of Cities to Visit

Before you travel, join a Facebook Group of the cities that you will visit. I joined one for Athens and people shared travel tips and pictures of Athens. It made me more aware of what I would see or what I wanted to see when I got to Athens.

Poem - Patriotic Day

Excitement and thrills
Thousands in the streets
Not marching to drills
And no drum beats

Hustling and bustling
Surging ahead
At first puzzling
I had a little dread

Then I noticed their flags

350

White and blue flags
Greek flags
Patriotic flags

Greek Independence Day
I had stumbled into their parade
They were celebrating in this fray
I became less afraid

Joining the crowds
Rolling my travel bags
We were moving like molasses
Drifting like clouds

I joined their dance
Heading for my hotel
We were heading that way by chance
My place to dwell

We marched right to it
And I jumped out
I hated to quit
But it was my route

No telling where it will stop
There were so many people
I saw the bellhop
And shot through the eye of the needle

Safely on the hotel steps
I looked back
And gave my respects
To this patriotic pack

So much pride
And reverence
What a great ride
All so adventurous

Acropolis

March 25, 2019, in Greece, Roman Agora
Acropolis - Paul told Athenians of One True God

Great Greek Lunch

March 25, 2019, in Greece, Syntagma square

Advice 48 – Ask Hotel Staff for Recommendations

I asked the hotel staff for the best Greek food in walking distance. They told me of a restaurant a few blocks which had the best Greek food. I took off for the restaurant because I was very hungry. The food was fabulous, and the hotel staff had made a great recommendation. See the picture below!

Ask the hotel staff for recommendations, they usually know the best places. Be more specific if you want an inexpensive place or a place where locals eat..

Prayer Wonderful Meal

Dear Father,

Thank you for providing this fabulous meal and all the meals you allow me. I thank you for giving me all I have in this world. You are my provider and protector. Thank you Lord.

In Jesus name I pray

Amen

Stoa Attalos

March 25, 2019, in Greece, Pnyx

Acropolis - Stadium

March 25, 2019, in Greece, Acrópolis of Athens

Wandering Athens

March 25, 2019, in Greece, Pnyx

Wandering Athens

March 25, 2019, in Greece, O Pirgos Ton Anemon

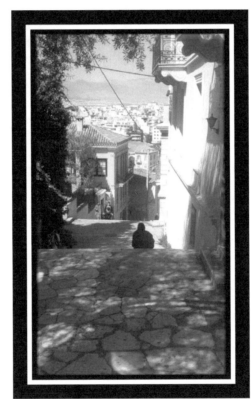

Athens Skyline

March 25, 2019, in Greece, Thiseio metro station Views from Acropolis and Phillopapou Hill

Athens Sunset

March 25, 2019, in Greece, Filopappou Hill

Prayer Sunset

Dear God,

All I see is your kingdom and your majesty in these sunsets.
You are creator of everything, and I stand in awe. Thank you
for this moment.

In Jesus name I pray

Amen

I never tire of a romantic sunset.

Poem Sunset

I have seen plenty
From places everywhere
Never too many
There is nothing to compare

I will never forget
The one on Filopappou Hill

The best yet
What a thrill

I wandered above Athens Acropolis
Following groups with picnic lunches
Venturing out from the metropolis
I had my hunches

They knew something special
So I followed close
And we climbed to a higher level
How high who knows

But we were way above
Athens and the surrounding cities
And I could feel the love
People picnicking and reminding me of hippies

There were youngsters
And bottles of wine
In small groups and clusters
Sitting down to dine

As the sun set
Over the skyline
I will never forget
The sun decline

Slow and sure
The sun shrunk
And there was no cure
As the sun sunk

It was marvelous
More than spectacular
A true armistice
For a battler

Why can we not remember
And memorize

As a world member
This godly prize

So beautiful
And relaxing
Strife is unsuitable
And war taxing

Look at this glory
And appreciate it
I want this to be my story
As I act out by life skit

Tranquil and dignified
Not bothering anyone
I do not want to backslide
Just to be with the One

The one who created this
And gave it to us
I do not want to miss
The Godly bus

Take me to heaven
When I die
Accession
To be with the One on High

Day 23 Athens

Wading in the Aegean Sea

March 26, 2019, in Greece, Ákra Ágios Kosmás

Poem Sunrise

I never get enough

Of the early morn sun
Most people huff
Sleep not done

But for me it is different
I am alive
So I am deliberate
To get up by five

Get a cup of coffee
Wander out to a grand place
Sometimes with a posse
Or just me at my pace

Sunrise from a sailboat
Sunrise from a beach
Sunrise from a building
Sunrise form a mountain

Does not matter where
Or for how long
Each sunrise is rare
And it sings a pretty song

The splendor of the orangeness
And then the red and yellow
Blending beyond barrenness
Into something very mellow

And then the yellow sphere
Creeps over the horizon
With a great cheer
The sun has risin

We have another day
To live and to make right
I want to be happy and gay
While the sun is so bright

Filling the sky

With more and more light
The sun is not shy
It is so bright

This is how I want my life
Shining and new
With no strife
And no witches brew

Just contentment
With what I got
No resentment
For what I have not

Athens's Summary

Historical Greece stands erect here. The erect historical buildings and monuments from ancient Greece litter Athens. They are all within walking distance but there are great public trolley's throughout the city and to the Adriatic Sea.

There is a bazaar and shops to rummage through. Many good restaurants to enjoy.

I think Athens will always be a city to revisit and to enjoy. I week or two would be tremendous to explore the city thoroughly.

Barcelona

Missed Barcelona

March 26, 2019, in Spain, Barcelona Sants Railway Station

The plane was late. I rode the metro for 40 minutes and I ran out of time. I wanted to visit the beach, but it will have to wait until another time.

Poem - Cities Missed

My plans go awry
Missing a city here and there
No reason to cry
It was extremely rare

A snowstorm or two
My only flight delayed
No reason to be blue
Lemons to lemonade

I stayed longer in some cities
I saw towns that I did not plan to see
I did not miss much my pretties
As I toured Europe like a banshee

Hooping and hollering
In twenty three cities and towns
Thirteen countries conquering
There had to be a few breakdowns

Nothing can be perfect
And expect the unexpected
To reduce any conflict
And to keep your sanity protected

I rolled with the punches
Adjusting my timetables
There were crunches

But this creates fantastic fables

Stuck in a snowstorm
Outside a train station
It was hard to stay warm
For a few hours duration

Broken trains
Three to be exact
Caused all sorts of pains
But it is a fact

These mishaps are memorable
I would not want it any other way
I felt commemorable
For saving each day

Day 24 Madrid

Madrid

Madrid is a city of rich history dating back hundreds of years. The city was founded by Muslim Moors who were eventually conquered and evicted from the country.

The Spaniards were adventures colonizing the new world and creating trade routes to and from Europe. They became quite wealthy. Madrid is the political and cultural hub of Spain. Madrid is an important city in Europe.

Madrid is gigantic city with many beautiful boulevards and parks. I got off the train and took a subway to the airport where my hotel was located. I checked in and had a late dinner. I went back to Madrid proper the next morning and I set off down Gran Via Which is the main street in Madrid.

Advice 49 – Ask the Hotel for Upgrades

I ask at every hotel can I have an upgrade to a bigger room, a better view, or a larger bed. In this case, I asked the hotel for an upgrade, and I went from a twin bed to a king bed. What a nice upgrade.

If you do not ask then you never know what you will get.

Poem - Madrid

I wandered Madrid
Enjoying the sights
Believing I am El Cid
A beloved Spanish knight

Fighting not for blood
But time
A tourist stud
Searching and seeking in rhyme

373

So much to see
For two days of travel
And I was free
At my pace to unravel

All of the great destinations
Sitting in courtyards and plazas
Sipping coffee on vacation
Recalling all Spains mighty causes

Fighting Muslims invaders
Discovering the new world
Subduing the English pirates and raiders
Surviving Fascism as it whirled

Spain had endured
From good times to bad
Unsecured to secured
Moving past the dictatorship fad

Reminding me of Don Quixote escapades
One of my favorite operas and books
He is fighting villains on his crusade
There is more going on than it looks

He is fighting a noble fight
To stay pure and true
A beacon of light
And a strong bond or glue

To the noblest of ideals
For all of the needy and depressed
You must hear his appeals
To be brave and pass the test

True to goodness
True to the humanity
True to the truth
True to God

Anything is possible
If you give it your best
Possible and best is compossible
With a holy quest

A holy quest for what is right
Maybe not popular
Pushing back the blight
As a holy swashbuckler

My mind ran through these thoughts
As I sat at Don Quixotes statue
And I was happy to bear the cross
And I remembered and knew

It should all be for God
The number one thing
And it is hard not to be a fraud
But you must cling to the King

No matter what
Or under any circumstance
You know it in your gut
Take a holy stance

For your friends and neighbors
For the born and unborn
God will reward your labors
And you will be reborn

Hop-On and Off Bus

March 27, 2019, in Spain, Puerta del Sol
Lazy travel but good when discombobulated.

Wandering Madrid

March 27, 2019, in Spain, Puerta del Sol

Catherdral de la Almudena

March 27, 2019, in Spain, Almudena Cathedral

Plaza de Mayor

March 27, 2019, in Spain, Plaza Mayor of Madrid
Sunning and coffee

Advice 50 – Observe People Around You

I enjoy watching people both locals and tourist. I think families with kids are hilarious remembering the days when I would haul my kids around tourist sights. They could be elated to grumpy, and it seemed always hungry.

The best way to watch and observe people is to sit back at a café, park or plaza and enjoy a beverage and soak up the atmosphere. I do this in every city, and it is one of my happiest memories.

Palacio Real

March 27, 2019, in Spain, El Jardín del Príncipe de Anglona

Don Quixote Statue

March 27, 2019, in Spain, Spanish square
Favorite story

Prayer Don Quixote

Dear Righteous One,

I am delighted to see this statue and to remember to book and movie. Thank you Lord for presenting such a foolish but righteous man to the world. He is determined to do everything in your glory. I hope I can remember that truism.

In Jesus name I pray

Amen

Cortes Ingles View

March 27, 2019, in Spain, Cuartel General del Ejercito del Aire

This is a department store in Madrid with a very good restaurant on the roof. It has fabulous views of Madrid. I highly recommend venturing here.

More Madrid Wandering

March 28, 2019, in Spain, Puerta del Sol

Madrid's Summary

This visit seemed so much different than the other cities. A cross between an expired empire and a romantic experience. There are many parks, plazas, and gardens to visit. I walked from one to the another in my two days visiting. I sat back and enjoyed the sun and drank cups of coffee in the plazas. Too much fun with plenty of time to think.

I need to go back and to jump into all it has to offer. Madrid has many experiences waiting to enjoy, and two days does not do it justice. I want to go back and to explore it more.

Day 26 New York

New York

I got off the plane and I went to the subway to go to my hotel. What a horrible scene at the subway station with people screaming and cursing. I did not hear anything like this all over Europe. There was not a police officer in sight. Finally, my subway car got there, and I was off. I felt more endangered in the subway in New York then anywhere in Europe.

Advice 51 – Splurge on a Taxi

When you are unsure of your circumstances, splurge on a taxi. Play it safe!

Prayer New York

Dear Holy One,

Thank you for reminding me that we do not live in a safe world and their our people in need of your love. I hope you continue to use me to share the gospel. I hope you allow me to be your servant. Thank you for any opportunities that you may place in front of me and may I react with understanding and kindness. You are God.

In Jesus name I pray

Amen

Poem - New York

After my European adventure
Arriving in New York
I felt that I needed a super avenger
For there was tremendous torque

A whirling force
At the airport subway
After leaving the concourse
I felt like prey

Crazies
Roaming the platform
And they were not picking daisies
But creating a nasty storm

Yelling and screaming
Condemnation and cursing
Was I daydreaming
Not traditional conversing

For thirty days
I have not encountered such crudeness
Some patrons had a craze
And unnecessary crudeness

Profanity littering the air
Threatening all within earshot
I offered up a prayer
Hopefully for naught

I had been in 20 or more train terminals
All over Europe
Where was the department of health and services
I was waiting for a flair up

Mentally ill
Or seeking attention
It made my blood chill
There was so much tension

I was scared
And embarrassed
These people were impaired
And not Americas fairest

They were thugs
Roaming the crowd
Maybe on drugs
Why was this allowed

But only in the United States
This is your welcoming
A bunch of inmates
Very troublesome and meddling

Your first impression
Reinforcing a stigma
America is not heaven
An enigma

America offers so much hope
And so many opportunities
But in this instance it is a kaleidoscope
Showing our communities and impurities

My train left the airport
And it was quiet again
Avoiding a blood sport
My nervousness began to drain

Off to the hotel
A fort of sorts
In a protective shell
Away from Americas warts

New York - World Trade Center

March 29, 2019, in the United States, National 9/11 memorial World Trade Center - a tragedy.

I cannot forget the second plane hitting the second World Trade Tower and I knew we were going to war. This was not an accident. The terror kept on and on all day with people jumping for their lives and they towers collapsing. A sad day in United States history.

Advice 52 – Pay Homage to National Tragedies

I find it a special memory to visit a memorial or a place where this was a national tragedy. The event is important to you and your nation and by visiting the location it reinforces the lost lives and historical significance of the event. For many it can be very emotional and upsetting but sometimes it is just a recognition of how important that place and event was in your life and your nation's destiny.

Wandering New York

March 29, 2019, in the United States, Nomad

New York is hectic and it can be unnerving trying to find your way around. I think I got lost twice especially trying to figure out the subway system.

Empire State Building

March 29, 2019, in the United States, WBLS-FM (New York) Icon

I can image King Kong climbing the Empire State Building with World War I biplanes buzzing and shooting at him. An iconic building for generations.

New York's Summary

New York is like Paris and the name speaks for itself. I have been to New York many times and it has endless places to visit. One day will never be enough and probably not a week or month.

I need to keep visiting and seeing it one or two days at a time.

Flying Home New York to St Louis to Jackson

March 29, 2019, in the United States, Lambert-St. Louis International Airport

Prayer Home Safe

Dear God,

I give thanks to you. I am home safe and sound. I have seen Europe and I have seen your creation. I enjoyed the churches and the Christian trails that I followed along my journey. You are wonderful to let me see these in my lifetime. Thank you Lord for a wonderful trip. Please forgive me of my sins and let me spend eternity with you.

In Jesus name I pray

Amen

Epilogue

This was the best trip that I have ever been on in my life. I saw so many wonderful places that I read about in school and seen in movies. I think one of my benefits was I was by myself. I did not have anyone else to worry about or to please. I think this made a huge difference in the quality of my trip.

I do not have a life ending disease, but there is something wrong with me. One doctor said my cognitive brain has separated from my emotional brain and there are triggers that make my symptoms worse. It is like shell shock which was caused by a traumatic injury which I have had a few. Over the past five years, I have stopped chasing a solution or remedy and I have lived my life.

I cannot do what I like in the business world, and I am not good around crowds of people. I am unable to negotiate or engage in heated arguments or stress. The weather has a role to play especially low humidity. But you find a way and you do the best that you can.

I am living in Orlando; Florida and I am sailing and writing. I have written a number of poetry books and a few bicycle travel guides. I want to write a novel and I have started two but I just do not get them done. This is one of the biggest goals left for me to fulfill.

Yes, I want to return to Europe especially Greece and southern Italy. I found these areas very satisfying and exhilarating. Someday, we will see.

About the Author

Conrad Birmingham is a businessman who is retired, and he is trying to stay busy. He has no natural talent at writing any type of writing except Quality Assurance Programs, Business Plans, Bible Study Notes, Business Price Quotes, Business Memos, Loan Requests, Consulting Reports, and all things business.

He has written poems for the past fifteen years. He has written four books of poetry, seven travel books, and he hopes you will enjoy reading them.

Conrad likes to share where he has been and to show how easy it can be. He loves to ride bicycles in major cities and to sail. He sails around Florida with plans to head toward the Bahamas one season. He is writing a book about sailing around Florida.

Conrad writes poetry to express himself. Conrad likes four stanzas with rhyming verses. They are called Quatrains, but he does not care. They are poems with four lines that rhyme. Also, he does not like punctuation. He does not use punctuation, allowing the verses to flow as they flow. He wants the reader to figure it out, and there are no participation trophies here.

The grand challenge is to write a novel, but this has alluded Conrad so far. He has started a few but cannot finish them. This is one of his main goals.

He hopes you enjoy his writings, and he wishes you to visit his website, conradwriter.com, and Facebook page, https://www.facebook.com/profile.php?id=100071070078910. He would like for you to leave comments and reviews. He encourages you to ask him questions about his writings. Good or bad, he does not mind. He wants to get better at writing, and he believes the best way is to be criticized and pushed to be better.

Appendix List of Travel Advice

Advice 1 – Plan Your Trip in Detail

I listed all the cities that I wanted to travel to and to explore. I studied the railroad maps in detail researching which ones had night cars traveling for 6 hours or more from one city to another city so I could sleep on the train. This was a key part of my journey. I learned a great deal preparing for this trip and it paid off the entire trip.

I learned that I could not get to Greece easily on the railroad, so I took a ferry from Bari, Italy to Patras, Greece. In reverse it was hard getting out of Greece, so I flew from Athens, Greece to Barcelona, Spain.

The second thing I learned was Greece's rail system was part of a rail pass, but you could not reserve seats because of Greece's economic troubles. There was nothing I could do about it, but it gave me some foresight on problems which might arise, and they did arise. Really, it was fun and exciting. More about that later when we reach Greece in the book.

Advice 2 – Purchase a European Rail Pass

The European Rail Pass enables you to travel on a train anywhere in Europe for one fee for a certain number of trips and days. This enabled you to make reservations ahead of time, so you knew that you had a seat, and you had a sleeper car. I was confused on which European Rail Pass was best, I chose eurail over raileurope. The main reason was eurail website was easier to use and understand. The prices were simpler.

Advice 3 – Pay for First Class

This was the best decision that I made on my trip. First Class allows you to sit in better seats with more amenities. The greatest amenity was charger's outlets for your phone. My phone needed to be constantly charged because of the posts that I was making on Facebook and Penguin (travel tracker), the usage of my maps to get around the cities, the internet to find interesting restaurants and historical sites, and the quantity of pictures that I was taking in each city. A few more amenities were free stacks in first-class, first-class restrooms (less people using them), and a better food menu then the regular train menu.

Advice 4 – Clothes

You must take limited clothes because you must carry them everywhere you go on the train. At the train depots there are lockers to place a suitcase into for the day, which is convenient, but you still must haul everything on and off the train. I took my favorite old man corduroy pants for warmth, a good pair of hiking boots, and good socks. I went in late winter in some countries and early spring in others. I rather be warm then cold. Pack one travel suitcase to leave in the train depot lockers and a good backpack to haul around as you toured the cities. This worked perfectly for me.

Advice 5 – Travel App

I used Penguin, a travel app, to document my trip. I posted pictures and stories about my trip. My friends could follow me on my trip. The app kept up with my location from my phone GPS. This created a great map of my trip. Also, at the end of the trip, I could print a book of my posts and pictures corresponding to the locations. I thought it was a great app and a provided great memory of my trip.

Advice 6 – Google Flights

There are so many advantages to using discount air apps to locate good inexpensive flights. Google Flight sis one of the best but make sure you search in incognito mode. You do not want to be tracked and pay more than you have to for tickets.

Advice 7 – Public Transportation Cards

In most major cities, you can purchase a mass transit pass to pay for the trips. Usually it will save you money, but it is very convenient to have an easy payment system instead of carrying the right cash and change. Also, you can jump from metro systems to buses very easy with the mass transit cards. You must purchase them in every city it is so much easier.

Advice 8 – City Map Apps

This is anither innovation thanks to smart phones. Download city map apps to your phone as soon as possible. They are connected to mass transportaion and tourist sites. If you are walking, it makes seeing al of the historical sites simple.

Advice 9 - Bicycles

A bicycle is the best way to see any city. There are bicycle trails, and you can move around the city from tourist location to tourist location. Most cities have bicycles that you can rent right from a rack, or you can telephone a bicycle shop. The bicycle shops will deliver them to you at a hotel or a specific location. I cannot emphasis how much fun it is to ride a bicycle as you tour a city.

Advice 10 – Use your Debit or Credit Card to Pay

Most debit and credit cards will convert from a foreign currency to the dollar. It is easier for you to pay the bill in the local currency with your bank card instead of carrying the foreign currency or letting the local establishment set the exchange rate. It is higher than normal.

Advice 11 – Hop On and Off Tour Buses

Hop on and off tour buses are an excellent way to see a city if you have little time or if you want an overview of the city. They give a good tour of the city with plenty of historical references and explanations.

Advice 12 – Get as High as You Can

Find the tallest building or hill I the city and go there. You get the best views of the city and usually it is breath taking.

Advice 13 – Take Plenty of Pictures

You want to take as many pictures as you can especially since they do not have to be developed and printed by the roll. I know kids do not get this, but it was a hassle and expensive. I am amazed at the pictures that I have created and the wonderful scenes and scenery. Just snap picture after picture and wait to find out what you have captured digitally. At night, I would go through my pictures eliminating the bad ones or duplicates.

Advice 14 – Pick Up Snacks at a Market

I recommend purchasing snacks at a local market that you may pass. Snacks can be expensive in train stations and on trains and many times not available or food establishments not open. Also, if you are wandering a city it is easier to snack on something handy in your backpack instead of stopping for a meal.

Advice 15 - Download Maps for City on to Cellphone

I had a map of the city, but it was not in detail. It gave the major attractions and bicycle route but not every street, so it got to be confusing. Next time, I will download most city maps on my cellphone so I have a map available if I do not have wi-fi or the map is inferior to what I need.

Advice 16 – Ask Directions

I was riding my bicycle to the river and I missed a turn. I rode twenty minutes further then I was supposed to go but I was lost. I could not figure out how to get to the river by the map and I was going to have to back track a long way to find the right path.

I asked a kid on the bicycle if he knew the way to the river. We had a hard tie communicating but he waved for me to follow him. He took me to the river, and it had to be out of his way. He was such a nice kid. He was so generous with his time.

Sometimes just ask directions instead of being frustrated and lost.

Advice 17 – Get a Cellphone Sims Card

I purchased a cellphone Sims card in Amsterdam for Europe. I did not get it in London because their sim cards were for Great Britain or Brussels because I did not feel safe there, but try to get it as soon as you can. Also, I had a dual sim card cellphone, so I plugged the second sim right into my cellphone. I was able to use the internet for directions a lot easier than finding a wi-fi spot. The sim card was very inexpensive.

Advice 18 – ATM's for Cash

In today's society, you do not have to carry a hefty sum of cash because there are ATM's everywhere where you can get cash. It is better than hiding your cash in a sock. Before you leave home, make sure you have a no fee bank card.

Advice 19 - Visit Tourism Office

Every city has a tourism office, and it is a good idea to visit theses offices. They usually have maps and lists of walking tours, bus tours, and other tours. Also, they have free advice, and they are knowledgeable about their city and what tourist like to do. This is a good place to start when you get to a city.

Advice 20 - Take Pictures of Luggage

You need a picture of your luggage. I did not lock my locker correcting in the Berlin train terminal and it was turned into lost and found. They were worried someone will steal it and I am glad for these good citizens.

I was able to show lost and found my luggage picture and it reduced the hassles of telling them what was inside my luggage – shirts, underwear, etc..

Advice 21 – Take a Walking Tour

A walking tour is an effective way to visit the main tourist sights and to learn a great deal about the city. They are available many times per day, and it will give you a good orientation and background of the city.

Advise 22 - Be Flexible

Something is going to go wrong no matter how hard you plan. My night train was cancelled due to the snow. I had to think quick and rearrange my route to get around the snow and to stay somewhat on track. I had to take two trains to get to my next stop but there was no sleeping car. I had planned to sleep but it is very difficult sitting in a second class train seat. I had to be flexible to get to my next stop and it was my only choice. I had no place to stay but on the trains.

I laid on two or three seats because no one was in the compartment with me. I woke up a few hours later and there were three people sitting across from me and another coming into the compartment to grab one of the seats I was lying on. How embarrassing. Be flexible.

Advice 23 - Make Copies of Passport

When you cross into Switzerland, they will take your passport. The conductor will return your passport but make a copy of your passport just in case. It is unnerving not to have your passport in your possession, but a copy will give you some comfort.

Advice 24 – Bring Good Walking Shoes

I planned to ride a bicycle mostly, so I did not have to walk as much, but Zurich was the exception. I walked everywhere for hours. I did not have walking shoes but boots. In hind sight, I wish I had brought one pair of walking shoes, but I did not think I had space for them – very foolish.

Advice 25 – Patience

I learned to be more patient in these cities especially when I first got off the train. Most of the rail stations are in the older parts of the city where it seems to be poorer and more run down. This is the first thing that I saw, and it gave me a false impression of the city. Remain patient and do not judge until the end.

Advice 26 – Free Wi-Fi

The best place to get free wi-fi is Starbucks. You can depend upon charging you phone at a Starbucks. A second wonderful place is the city libraries.

Advice 27 – Get Lost

I got lost walking from the train station to the old city of Warsaw. I was surprised at the things that I got to see while lost. I saw beautiful monuments off the beaten track and beautiful buildings in many different architectural style. If you get lost, then look for the good and the unexpected in each city.

Advice 28 – Say Yes

I took a taxi from the old city of Warsaw to the ghetto portion of Warsaw. My taxi driver said he would haul me around the ghetto neighborhood for ten dollars. I was leery of this guy because he asked me too many questions about where I was staying and who I was with. Also, I felt he was trying to pick me up wanting to know if we could get dinner together and he would take me to the train station. A bit unusual, but I said yes to him giving me a tour of the ghetto area but no to the rest. He took me to the ghetto going down back alleys and showing me the old ghetto walls and explain ways the kids got in and out of the ghetto smuggling supplies in and out. It was a great tour.

You have to say yes sometime to see sights that are not part of the usual tours.

Advice 29 – Act Like a Tourist

In some cities, it is best to act like a tourist. People can be friendly and extremely helpful. I entered int more conversations when I asked about a monument or asked how to get to a tourist location. Most of the time, I said I am tourist and I am lost can you help me. I think it did help me.

Advice 30 – Portable Power Bank Charger

I found using my cellphone all day for travel directions and pictures it would drain the battery down near empty. If I was staying in a hotel, it was no problem to plug my cellphone in to wall socket and recharge it. But, when you are moving from city to city on a train there is nowhere to charge your cellphone.. It is a problem.

A portable power bank charger or two is a necessary to keep your cellphone charged for directions or entertainment.

Advice 31 – Read A History Book

I knew nothing about Milan. Next time, I will read a history book about Milan. When you know more about places you are visiting it makes it much more exciting and rememberable.

I did read about Thessalonica, so I remember more form that visit then I do in Milan. Also, I know the books of the New Testament, Acts, Corinthians, and Thessalonians and when I visited those cities it was relevant to my knowledge.

Read about the cities before you go.

Advice 32 – Eat the Street Food

There were food vendors around the castle and many people were flocking to these food vendors. I decided to get something to eat from one of the food carts. The food was hot and delicious. I got a good portion of food, and the price was very reasonable. It made a great picnic looking at the massive walls on a bright sunny day.

Advice 33 – Carry Ear Plugs and Eye Mask

I have been traveling on night train cars where you share a room with four strangers. I have done that two or three times, but this time it was quite different. A lady came into our compartment with a baby. The baby was crying, and she said this was her bunk with the baby. I was so, so happy that I had my ear plugs and my eye mask. I jumped into my bunk and put on ear plugs and eye mask and went right to sleep. I could faintly hear the baby crying. Ear plugs and eye mask are necessary on night trains – be warned!

Advice 34 – City Attraction Cards

A good bargain to go into various attractions and sometimes to get discounts on transportation purchase a city discount card. The price of entry to a large number of museums and other attractions can be quite expensive but with you get a good discount purchasing a city discount card. A bonus is access to discounted public transportation such as subways and buses.

Advice 35 – Keep Your Guard Up

In any city or crowded circumstances keep your guard up. I was leaving the subway on the way to the Eiffel Tower, and I was on a one person, very tight escalator. I noticed two you adults rushing up behind me pushing past people and there was nowhere for them to go because the escalator was full of people.

One of the young men bumped hard into me and pushed past me while the second guy tried to pick my wallet out of my back pocket. My wallet was no there so I was not worried so I turned around and said excuse me with a stare. They took off up the escalator pushing their way through the crowd.

Keep your guard up these things happen all over the world.

Advice 36 – Eat like the Locals

I went to subway early in the morning and I was hungry. I watched the locals go up to the food counter and they ordered an espresso and a loaf of bread. They drank the expresso like a shot downing it in one gulp and took off with their bread for breakfast.

I ordered the same thing just like a Parisian. It was fun watching the people and their local customs. I recommend watching what the locals are eating and drinking and then partake of what they are eating. It will be a grand memory of your trip and you will not go wrong.

Advice 37 - Eat Main Meal for Lunch

I ate my main meal for lunch for a number of reasons and in Florence it was no difference. I had trouble meeting my landlord, so I stopped and I ate lunch at a restaurant near my flat. I used the time to review what I was going to do next. The food was delicious, and they have a lower price for lunch just like most places in the world. I got a rest, I got reorganized, I waited for someone, and I saved money.

Advice 38 – Universal Travel Adaptor

I had no problems with charging my cellphone in most cities but not in Florence. The wall outlets were old fashion, just like my flat. I had to skip charging my cellphone this night. Pack a universal travel adaptor for emergencies.

Advice 39 – Be Respectful

I was at the train station at the end of the day, and I was going to take a train out of Rome roughly fifteen miles to a smaller town just to experience Italy in a unique way. I asked where the line was for the train and the train staff told me over there. I waited in line twenty to thirty minutes, and they told me I was in the wrong line and to go to that line. I went to that line and after I got to the counter, I missed my train. I asked to go to another town, and they said my ticket would not do that. I got mad and argued with the train staff asking for the manager. I looked like a stupid buffoon or an angry tourist. Probably like a spoiled American. I needed to be more patient and respectful, it was no big deal. I learned my lesson.

Advice 40 – Early Bird

I learned a long time ago; you have to get up and to get moving before the crowds appear. This is true for shopping and for touring. It was truer in Rome. I moved from one part of the city early in the morning without much difficulty but as the day wore on there were more and more people. The tourist attractions were more and more crowded along with the sidewalks. This is a truism – you have to be the early bird.

Advice 41 - Open Mind

I was in almost in a panic mode because there must of be thousands of kids all over the place. The streets were packed with teenagers, and it made me uncomfortable. The crowds were so tight, and it was hard to get around. I do not like crowds and pushy ones at that, so a bunch of teenagers are the pushiest. I buckled down and I kept an open mind. They are not here to harm anyone, they are here for a Eurozone event. I think it was something to do with the environment but never the less, I remembered why I was there. To tour the city just like these kids..

Advice 42 - Try New Food

I was in Bari, and I follow my own advice to eat my main meal at lunch so I can get reorganized and prepared for the rest of the day. I found a restaurant near the docks; I asked them to give me the best local food that they had available. It was seafood and it was fabulous. I did not ask what I was eating but it was octopus, and sea urchins. The best way to try new food is to ask for their local foods and eat it without complaint.

Advice 43 – Download Google Translate

In most of Europe, I found people spoke English or some type of broken English. It was not until I ventured into southern Italy, which is probably not a high tourist location for English speaking peoples that I seemed to have a greater language barrier. Google translate would have been very handy here in Bari.

I was unable to communicate with most of the local populace. I think the country of Italy was the hardest to communicate with in Europe. I had an easier time in Russia speaking to the Russians then the Italians.

Remember to download Google translate to make life easier.

Advice 44 – Be Open to Strangers

I say hello and I smile to everyone that I pass on my travels.. It is basic kindness and courtesy.

On this trip while I was wandering Thessaloniki, I was seeing the same women at all the tourist locations We were walking to the same locations for miles. I finally said hi and we chatted as we walked throughout the city. We spend the next few hours touring Thessaloniki together. It was fun having someone to talk to and to share the experience.

Take a chance and chat to strangers – say hello and smile.

Advice 45 – Haggle

In some countries it may be rude to ask for a lower price, but in many countries it is the custom. In Thessalonica's market, I would ask what your best price is or ask for twenty percent. Most of the time, we would get to ten percent.

There is a tremendous amount of fun in negotiating with the locals and many times it is expected of you.

Advice 46 – Spontaneity

Take a chance. Do something new. Going into the prayer houses was new for me. I have not seen these in the United States, so it was a shock that the prayer houses were on every corner. When you act spontaneous it is exciting and rememberable.

Advice 47 – Join a Facebook Group of Cities to Visit

Before you travel, join a Facebook Group of the cities that you will visit. I joined one for Athens and people shared travel tips and pictures of Athens. It made me more aware of what I would see or what I wanted to see when I got to Athens.

Advice 48 – Ask Hotel Staff for Recommendations

I asked the hotel staff for the best Greek food in walking distance. They told me of a restaurant a few blocks which had the best Greek food. I took off for the restaurant because I was very hungry. The food was fabulous, and the hotel staff had made a great recommendation. See the picture below!

Ask the hotel staff for recommendations, they usually know the best places. Be more specific if you want an inexpensive place or a place where locals eat..

Advice 49 – Ask the Hotel for Upgrades

I ask at every hotel can I have an upgrade to a bigger room, a better view, or a larger bed. In this case, I asked the hotel for an upgrade, and I went from a twin bed to a king bed. What a nice upgrade.

If you do not ask then you never know what you will get.

Advice 50 – Observe People Around You

I enjoy watching people both locals and tourist. I think families with kids are hilarious remembering the days when I would haul my kids around tourist sights. They could be related to grumpy, and they seemed always hungry.

The best way to watch and observe people is to sit back at a café, park or plaza and enjoy a beverage and soak up the atmosphere. I do this in every city and it is one of my happiest memories.

Advice 51 – Splurge on a Taxi

When you are unsure of your circumstances, splurge on a taxi. Play it safe!

Advice 52 – Pay Homage to National Tragedies

I find it a special memory to visit a memorial or a place where this was a national tragedy. The event is important to you and your nation and by visiting the location it reinforces the lost lives and historical significance of the event. For many it can be very emotional and upsetting but sometimes it is just a recognition of how important that place and event was in your life and your nation's destiny.

Made in the USA
Columbia, SC
14 January 2024

30435136R00226